# ESSENTIAL
## Skills and Practice
### Your all-in-one source for school success!

Thinking Kids®
An imprint of Carson-Dellosa Publishing LLC
Greensboro, North Carolina

Thinking Kids®
An imprint of Carson-Dellosa Publishing LLC
P.O. Box 35665
Greensboro, NC 27425  USA

ISBN  978-1-4838-0243-5

04-100177784

# Table of Contents

Name _____

# Sailing Away

Connect the dots from **A** to **Z**.

Name _____

# Let's Play Leapfrog

Help the girl find her way to the frog exhibit. Color the path in order from **N** to **Z**.

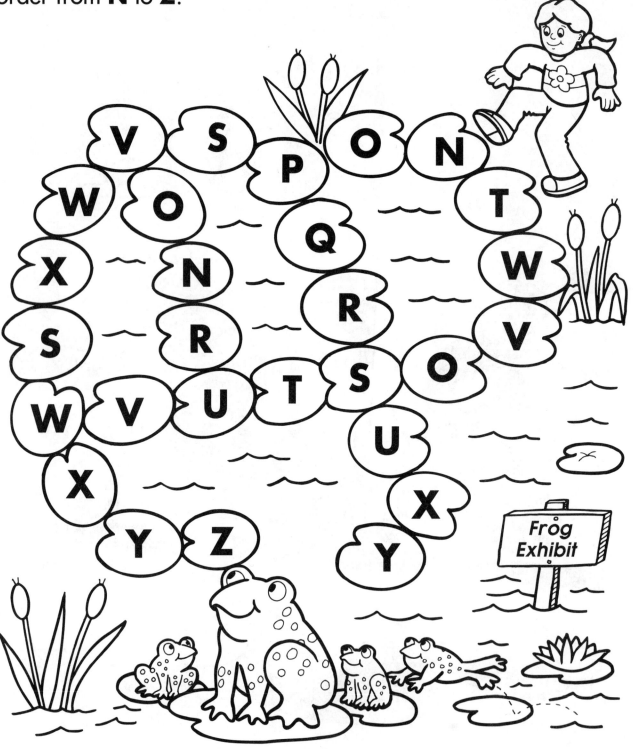

*Essential Skills and Practice Grade K*

Name _____

# Sailing Away

Follow the alphabet to lead the pig to the radio.

*Essential Skills and Practice Grade K*

Name _____

# Fantastic Farm

Find the letters from **a** to **m**. Color them.

## a b c d e f g h i j k l m

*Essential Skills and Practice Grade K*

Name _____

# Trace and Write

Trace the letters. Then write each letter.

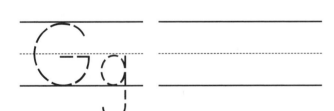

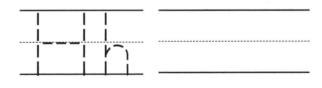

*Essential Skills and Practice Grade K*

Name _____

# Trace and Write

Trace the letters. Then write each letter.

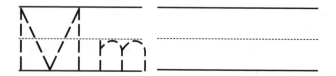

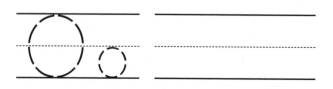

*Essential Skills and Practice Grade K*

Name _____

# Trace and Write

Trace the letters. Then write each letter.

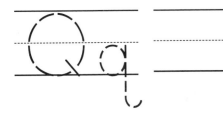 

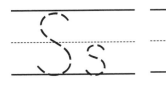 

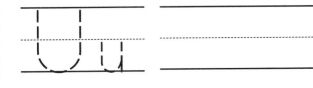 

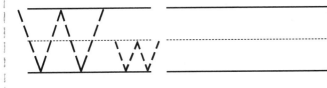 

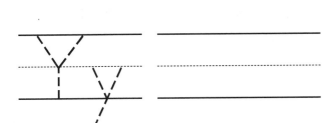 

*Essential Skills and Practice Grade K*

Name _____

# Letter Trucks

Write the letter that comes between.

*Essential Skills and Practice Grade K*

Name _____

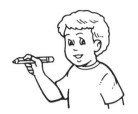

# Letter Matchup

In each row, circle the letters that match the first letter.

| B | B B R P |
|---|---|
| C | Q O C C |
| D | D P D O |
| F | P F E F |

Name _____

# More Matching

In each row, circle the letters that match the first letter.

| | |
|---|---|
| **b** | p b q b |
| **c** | c q o c |
| **d** | p d o d |
| **f** | p f t f |

*Essential Skills and Practice Grade K*

Name _____

# Letter Garden

Draw lines between the flowers to match the uppercase and lowercase letters.

Aa Bb Cc Dd Ee Ff Gg Hh Ii
Jj Kk Ll Mm Nn Oo Pp Qq Rr
Ss Tt Uu Vv Ww Xx Yy Zz

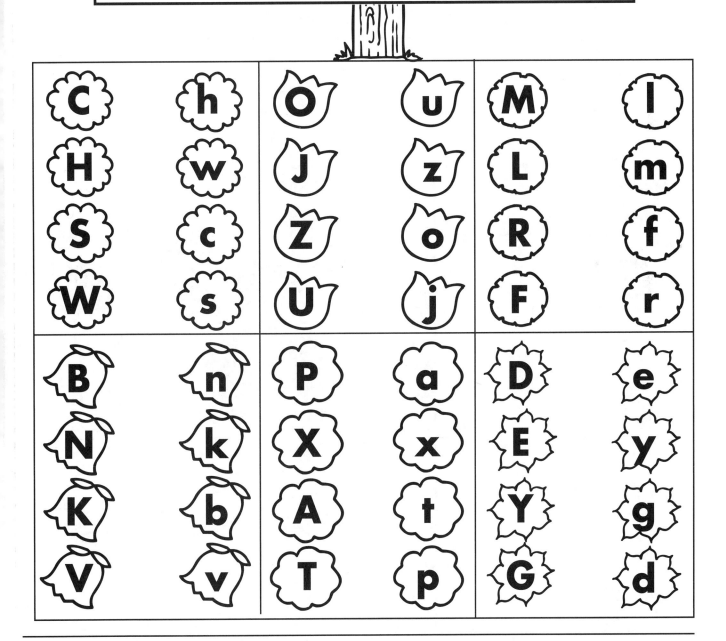

*Essential Skills and Practice Grade K*

Name _____

# I Can Match Letters

Draw a line from each child to the matching lowercase letter.

| a |
| m |
| g |

| l |
| w |
| r |

| q |
| l |
| r |

| g |
| s |
| m |

| k |
| o |
| t |

| n |
| d |
| i |

| l |
| o |
| h |

| e |
| z |
| p |

12

*Essential Skills and Practice Grade K*

Name _____

# Follow the Path

Say the alphabet. Write the missing letters.

*Essential Skills and Practice Grade K*

Name _____

# A Lost Ball

Help Tommy find his ball.
Follow the words in ABC order.

ape

hair

dog

egg

bunny

cab

cat

gift

fish

donkey

apple

nest

eating

gate

flower

*Essential Skills and Practice Grade K*

Name _____

# Hungry Birds

Help the birds find the worms.
Color the boxes in ABC order.

| | | ape | hug | fox |
|---|---|---|---|---|
| | | ball | star | gas |
| deer | cake | cut | door | leg |
| fan | lake | man | ear | fish |
| kite | jet | ice | land | goat |
| lips | king | joke | igloo | hat |
| map | bed | rose | net | kiss |
| nose | owl | pet | quit | |

*Essential Skills and Practice Grade K*

Name _____

# New Word Fun

Write the first letter for each picture.
Write the letters in the boxes to make a new word.

1.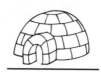

2.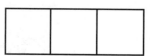

3.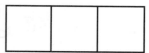

4.

*Essential Skills and Practice Grade K*

Name _____

# Fill Them In

Write the vowels to complete each word.

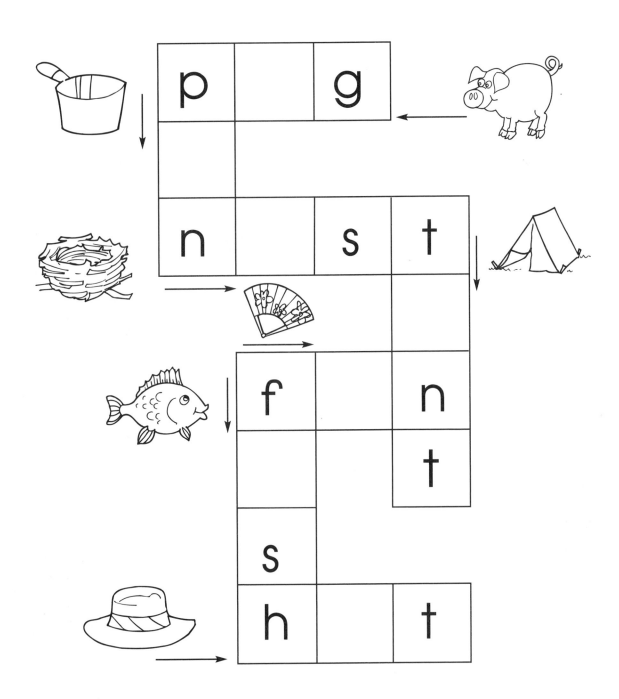

*Essential Skills and Practice Grade K*

Name _____

# The Sound of C

Draw a line from each cat to a picture that begins with the sound of **c**

## Write **Cc**.

C c   C c

*Essential Skills and Practice Grade K*

Name _____

# The Sound of G

Color the pictures that begin with the sound of **g**.

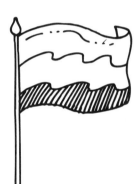

Write **Gg**.

*Essential Skills and Practice Grade K*

Name _____

# The Sound of L

Look at the living room. Draw a circle around five things that begin with the sound of **L**. Color the picture.

Write **Ll**.

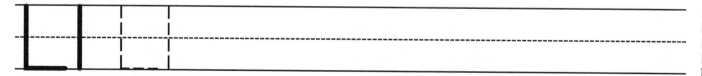

Name _____

# Rain, Rain, Go Away

Find these things, which begin with **m**. Color them brown. Then color the rest of the picture.

mouse

monkey

mop

milk

mask

*Essential Skills and Practice Grade K*

Name _____

# Water Lover

Find these things, which begin with **r**. Color them orange. Then color the rest of the picture

rose      rake      ring      rocket      raccoon

Name _____

# Plump Pig

Color each **u** purple. Then color the rest of the picture.

Name _____

# The Sound of Y

Look at each picture. If it begins with **y**, circle **yes**. If it does not, circle **no**.

   yes   no           yes   no

   yes   no           yes   no

   yes   no           yes   no

   yes   no           yes   no

Write **Yy**.

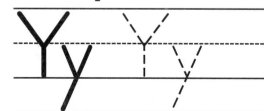

*Essential Skills and Practice Grade K*

Name _____

# All Kinds of Animals

Look at each animal. Say its name. Circle the sound you hear at the beginning of the word.

**l**　　**m**

**r**　　**d**

**c**　　**f**

**b**　　**g**

**j**　　**h**

**v**　　**w**

**x**　　**y**

**q**　　**z**

**r**　　**s**

**t**　　**v**

**h**　　**k**

**n**　　**p**

*Essential Skills and Practice Grade K*

Name _____

# Food Fun

Look at the first picture in each row. Say its name. Then color the picture that has the same beginning sound.

Name _____

# Listen Carefully

Look at each column. Color the pictures that begin with the letter shown at the top.

*Essential Skills and Practice Grade K*

Name _____

# Matching Sounds

Draw lines from each letter to the pictures with the same beginning sound.

*Essential Skills and Practice Grade K*

Name _____

# Floating High

Color the words that start with **e** orange.
Color the words that start with **f** yellow.
Write the words under the correct beginning letters below.

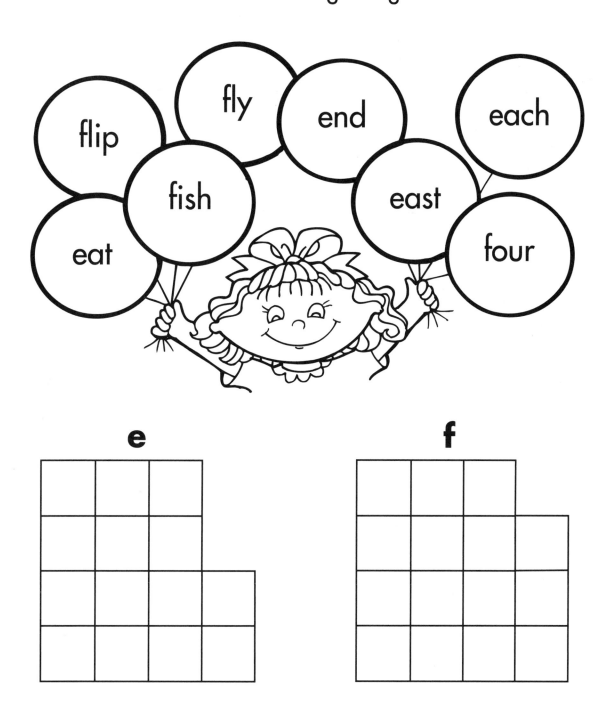

**e**

**f**

*Essential Skills and Practice Grade K*

Name _____

# Scrambled J's, K's, and L's

Unscramble the words that name the pictures.
Write the words.

1.  nkitet _____

2.  kngi _____

3.  mlap _____

4.  elg _____

5.  kiet _____

6. scajk _____

**Word Box**

kite

king

leg

jacks

kitten

lamp

Name _____

# Ending Sounds

Listen for the ending sound of each picture. Write it at the end of each word.

## ba

## bu

## cu

## he

## mu

*Essential Skills and Practice Grade K*

Name _____

# More Ending Sounds

Listen for the ending sound of each picture. Write it at the end of each word.

tu _____

be _____

fa _____

ca _____

to _____

pi _____

*Essential Skills and Practice Grade K*

Name _____

# Beginning and End

Say the names of the pictures. Write the letters that make the beginning and ending sounds.

_____
- - - - - - - - - - - - -
a
_____

_____
- - - - - - - - - - - - -
o
_____

_____
- - - - - - - - - - - - -
a
_____

_____
- - - - - - - - - - - - -
o
_____

_____
- - - - - - - - - - - - -
e
_____

_____
- - - - - - - - - - - - -
u
_____

*Essential Skills and Practice Grade K*

Name _____

# Discovering Differences

Circle the animal that is different in each column.

*Essential Skills and Practice Grade K*

Name _____

# Missing Parts

Some of these elephants are missing body parts! Look at elephant **A** to see what's missing on the others. Name the missing body parts and draw them on the animals.

**A**

**B**

**C**

**D**

*Essential Skills and Practice Grade K*

Name _____

# Parts and Wholes

Complete each picture by drawing the missing piece.

*Essential Skills and Practice Grade K*

Name _____

# What's Different?

Can you find and circle ten ways the bottom picture is different?

37          *Essential Skills and Practice Grade K*

Name _____

# Opposite Matchup

Draw lines to match the opposites.

*Essential Skills and Practice Grade K*

Name _____

# Ocean Opposites

Draw lines to match the opposites.

little

fast

out

sink

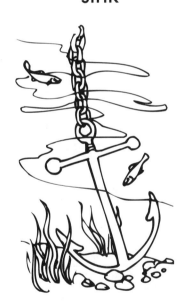

big

in

slow

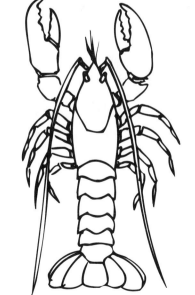

float

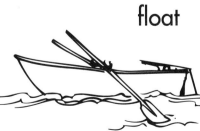

*Essential Skills and Practice Grade K*

Name _____

# Word Match

Match each word with a picture.

cat •

dog •

pan •

ball •

Name _____

# Fun Word Match

Match each word with a picture.

plane •

leaf •

bed •

nut •

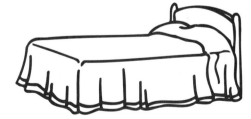

Name _____

# Matching Words

Circle matching pairs of words.

| | |
|---|---|
| go     go | sat     cat |
| fox     fox | at     to |
| top     toe | red     red |
| no     no | car     cat |

Name _____

# I Read Words

In each box, circle the words that match the word at the top.

| eat |
|---|
| eat      eat |
| cat      ear |

| play |
|---|
| play      pay |
| plan      play |

| yes |
|---|
| yet      yes |
| yes      you |

| take |
|---|
| tack      take |
| tan      take |

| me |
|---|
| me      met |
| men      me |

| work |
|---|
| walk      work |
| work      woke |

*Essential Skills and Practice Grade K*

Name _____

# Final Question

Match the scrambled letters to find out what the farmer wants to ask.

| | | | | ' | | | | | | | | | | | | | | | | |
|---|---|---|---|---|---|---|---|---|---|---|---|---|---|---|---|---|---|---|---|---|
| 1 | 2 | 3 | 4 | | 5 | | 6 | 7 | | 8 | 9 | 10 | | 11 | 12 | 13 | | 14 | 15 | 16 | | 17 | 18 | 19 | 20 | 21 |

Name _____

# A Plane

Write the sentence.

# See the plane go up.

_____

- - - - - - - - - - - - - - - - - - - - - - - - - - - - -

_____

Find and circle the words.
The words go across →
and down ↓.

| Word Box |
| --- |
| up |
| plane |
| See |
| go |
| the |

| g | S | e | e | n | p |
|---|---|---|---|---|---|
| h | l | s | t | v | l |
| q | g | z | f | r | a |
| b | o | m | e | c | n |
| z | r | k | u | p | e |
| t | h | e | z | o | w |

*Essential Skills and Practice Grade K*

Name _____

# Word Match

Circle the words that match the words at the top of each box.

| red sled |

red slide

red sled

| fun ride |

fun ride

fan ride

| wet kid |

well kid

wet kid

| hot fire |

hot fire

hot find

*Essential Skills and Practice Grade K*

Name _____

# A Secret Sentence

Color the following words in the puzzle **green**.

| camp | when | test | time |

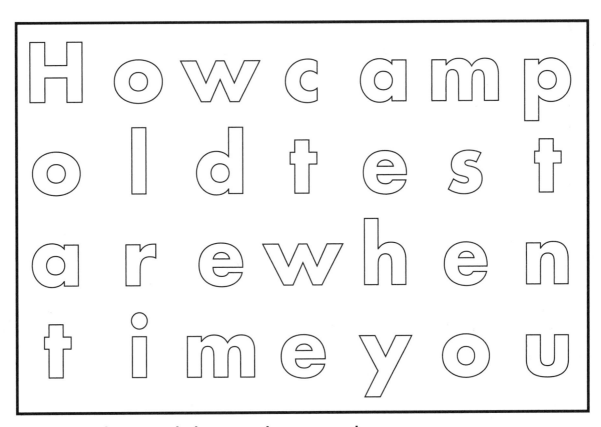

Write the words you did not color to make a sentence.

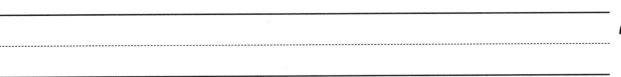

?

Name _____

# Look and Color

Color the following words red.

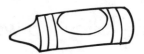

| the | was | on | and | but |
|-----|-----|-----|-----|-----|

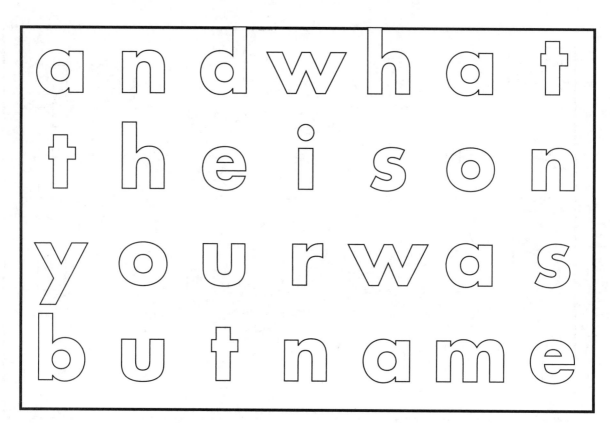

Write the words you did not color to make a sentence.

_____

------------------------------- **?**

_____

*Essential Skills and Practice Grade K*

Name _____

# New Words

Color the picture. Add the letter. Write the word.

| | | |
|---|---|---|
| | **p** | |
| | · ick | |
| | **l** | |
| | · ick | |
| | **k** | |
| | · ick | |
| | **s** | |
| | · ick | |

*Essential Skills and Practice Grade K*

Name _____

# Crack the Code

Write the missing letters for each word.
Use the code at the bottom of the page.

1. _____ _____ayon ○ ☆

2. _____ou_____e ⬠ △

3. _____oon ⬠

4. _____ta_____ △ ☆

5. _____lou_____ ○ ▢

6. _____a_____ _____ot ○ ☆ ☆

7. bi_____ _____ ☆ ▢

8. _____on_____ey ⬠ ◇

| c | ○ |
| r | ☆ |
| s | △ |
| m | ⬠ |
| d | ▢ |
| k | ◇ |

Name _____

# re Them Out

mble each word. Be sure that it matches the meaning.

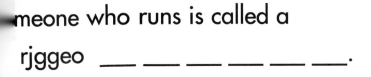

| | | |
|---|---|---|
| teacher | ice cream | apple |
| mouse | jogger | tennis |

meone who runs is called a

rjggeo  ___ ___ ___ ___ ___ ___ .

game that uses a racket and a small ball is

ıne  ___ ___ ___ ___ ___ ___ .

mething cold to eat on a hot day is

cie ramec  ___ ___ ___  ___ ___ ___ ___ ___ .

neone who teaches children is a

erhteac  ___ ___ ___ ___ ___ ___ ___ .

asty fruit that grows on a tree is called an

leppa  ___ ___ ___ ___ ___ .

urry little animal that squeaks is a

somue  ___ ___ ___ ___ ___ .

# Double Trouble

Write each word in the box next to a word in the p[u] new word.

| bell | walk | ground | ro[o] |
|------|------|--------|-------|
| box | ball | fish | pri |

1. | s | a | n | d | | | |

2. | s | i | d | e | | | |

3. | b | e | d | | | |

4. | s | t | a | r | | | |

5. | f | o | o | t | | | | |

6. | b | a | s | e | | | |

7. | d | o | o | r | | | |

8. | c | a | m | p | | | | |

# Fig[u]

Unscr[a]

1. S[c]

2. A

   sti

3. S[c]

4. So

5. A

6. A

Name _____

# Double Trouble

Write each word in the box next to a word in the puzzle to make a new word.

| bell | walk | ground | room |
| box | ball | fish | print |

1. | s | a | n | d | | | |

2. | s | i | d | e | | | |

3. | b | e | d | | | | |

4. | s | t | a | r | | | |

5. | f | o | o | t | | | | |

6. | b | a | s | e | | | |

7. | d | o | o | r | | | |

8. | c | a | m | p | | | | | |

Name _____

# Figure Them Out

Unscramble each word. Be sure that it matches the meaning.

| teacher | ice cream | apple |
|---------|-----------|-------|
| mouse | jogger | tennis |

1. Someone who runs is called a

   rjggeo ___ ___ ___ ___ ___ ___.

2. A game that uses a racket and a small ball is

   stinne ___ ___ ___ ___ ___ ___.

3. Something cold to eat on a hot day is

   cie ramec ___ ___ ___  ___ ___ ___ ___ ___.

4. Someone who teaches children is a

   erhteac ___ ___ ___ ___ ___ ___ ___.

5. A tasty fruit that grows on a tree is called an

   leppa ___ ___ ___ ___ ___.

6. A furry little animal that squeaks is a

   somue ___ ___ ___ ___ ___.

# At the Bus Stop

Read each question. Answer the question aloud.
Trace the question mark at the end of the question.

Why are the people waiting?

Who has groceries?

Who has a newspaper?

How many kids are waiting?

Name _____

# Is It a Question?

Read the sentence. Then repeat it. After repeating the sentence, tell whether it is a question or a statement.

1. My wagon is red.

2. The sky looks cloudy.

3. My favorite colors are red and blue.

4. Do you know where the store is?

5. Is this a difficult activity?

6. I am very tired today.

7. First I wake up and then I brush my teeth.

8. After school I like to play with my friends.

9. What time do you go to school?

10. He helped her ride the bike last Saturday.

Name _____

# Words

Write the correct word on each line.

I will go to a _____
_____
_____ .

pond

pool

food

We need some _____
_____
_____ .

rocks

menu

I want to read a _____
_____
_____ .

book

cat

I can help the _____
_____
_____ .

dog

*Essential Skills and Practice Grade K*

Name _____

# Color Craze

Follow the directions for each coloring activity.

1. Color the items you can eat.

2. Color the objects you write with.

3. Color the toys.

4. Color the fruit.

5. Color the capital letters.

B d y F i M

classifying

Name _____

# I Can Have Fun

Color the things that go together in each row.

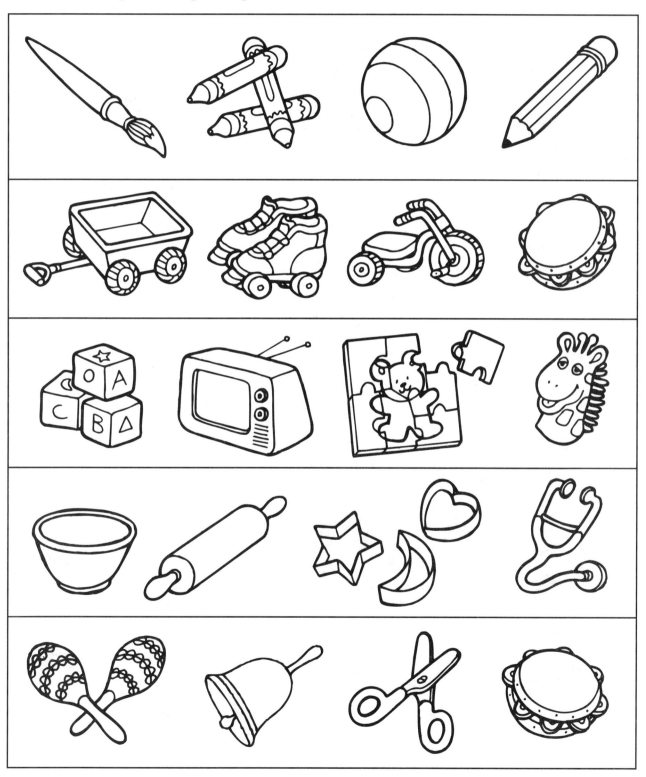

Name _____

# In the Middle

Color each object that is in the middle.

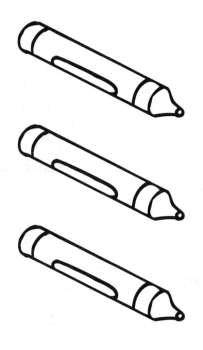 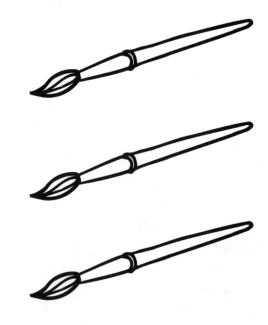

*Essential Skills and Practice Grade K*

Name _____

# Top, Middle, Bottom

Look at the picture. Who is at the **top** of the hill? Who is at the **middle** of the hill? Who is at the **bottom** of the hill? Fill in the blanks below.

The dog is at the _____ of the hill.

The cat is at the _____ of the hill.

The boy is at the _____ of the hill.

*Essential Skills and Practice Grade K*

Name _____

# In or Out

Look at each picture. Circle whether the clown is **in** or **out**.

in          out          in          out          in          out

in          out          in          out          in          out

Name _____

# Color Words

Say the color names. Color the pictures.

red

orange

yellow

green

blue

purple

black

brown

*Essential Skills and Practice Grade K*

Name _____

# What a Great day!

Read the color words. Color the spaces to match.

Name _____

# More Color Words

Trace the words. Say the color names. Color the crayons.

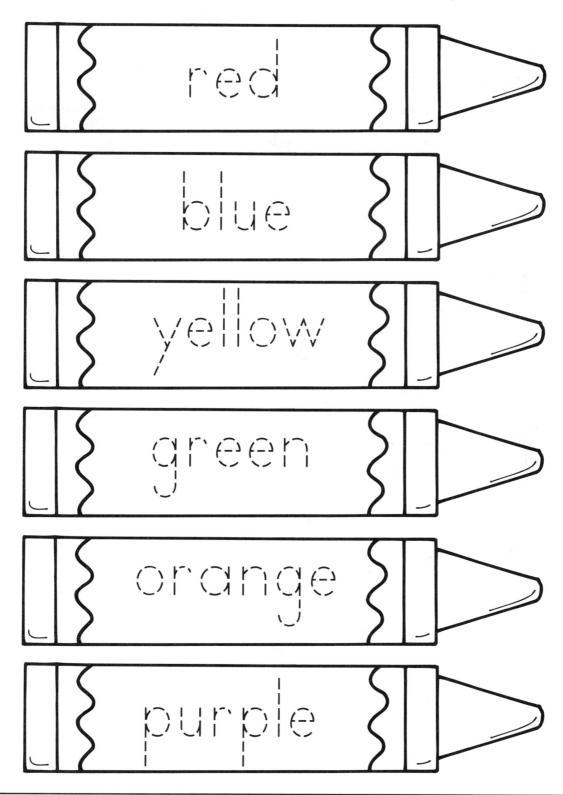

*Essential Skills and Practice Grade K*

Name _____

# A Tisket, a Tasket

Follow the directions to color the basket.
1. Color one flower red.
2. Color one flower blue.
3. Draw a bow on the basket.
4. Color the basket green and yellow.
5. Draw another flower in the basket.

64                                    *Essential Skills and Practice Grade K*

Name _____

# Make a Picture

Follow the directions to complete the picture.

1. Draw a tree to the right of the school.

2. Draw a sun in the top left of the picture.

3. Draw a flag to the left of the school.

4. Draw some flowers to the right of the tree.

5. Draw a picture of yourself to the left of the school.

Name _____

# I Enjoy Books

Circle and write the best title for the picture.

Eating Dinner

Books for Sale

We Like to Read

_____

- - - - - - - - - - - - - - - - - - - - - - - - - - - - - - - - -

_____

- - - - - - - - - - - - - - - - - - - - - - - - - - - - - - - - -

_____

Name _____

# Can It Really Happen?

Does each picture show something
that can really happen?
Circle **yes** if it does.
Circle **no** if it does not.

yes

no

yes

no

yes

no

yes

no

yes

no

yes

no

Name _____

# Funny Garden

Does each picture show something that can really happen?
Circle **yes** if it does.
Circle **no** if it does not.

   yes

no

   yes

no

   yes

no

   yes

no

   yes

no

   yes

no

*Essential Skills and Practice Grade K*

Name _____

# Rhyme Time

Color. Draw lines to match the rhyming words.

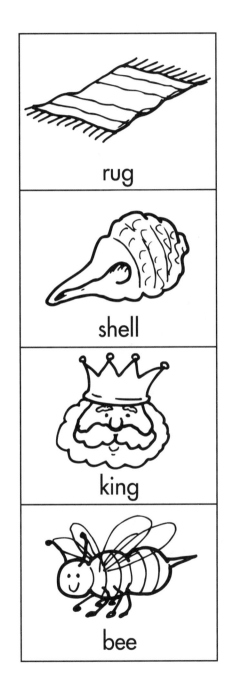

*Essential Skills and Practice Grade K*

Name _____

# Time to Rhyme

Use the picture clues to match the rhyming words.

1.  meat

2.  seal

3.  king

4.  mouse

5.  clock

6.  hair

7.  dog

8. boat

 sock

 wheel

 bear

 ring

 goat

 frog

 feet

house

Name _____

# Before and After

Look at the picture in the middle. Draw something that happens before and after. Trace the words.

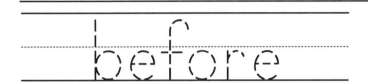

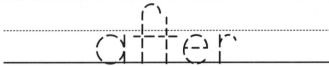

*Essential Skills and Practice Grade K*

Name _____

# Draw a Dinosaur

These pictures are out of order. Number the steps from 1 to 6.

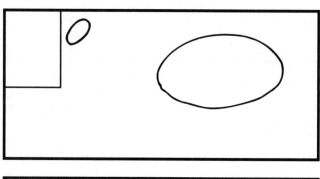 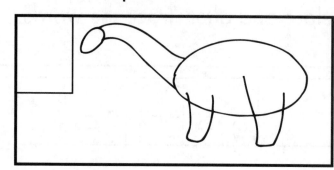

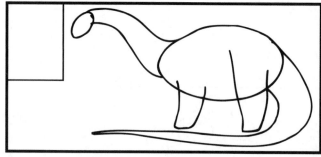 

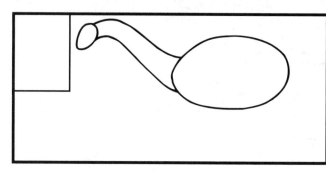 

Follow the steps to draw a dinosaur.

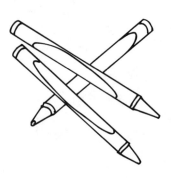

*Essential Skills and Practice Grade K*

Name _____

# My Day at Kindergarten

Read the story below. Then cut out and place the sentences in sequential order.

When the bell rings it is time to go inside. First, the teacher reads a story. Then we have a snack. Finally, we do an art project. At 12:00, it is time to go home.

 When the bell rings it is time to go inside.

 Then we have a snack.

 Finally, we do an art project.

 At 12:00 it is time to go home.

 First, the teacher reads a story.

Name _____

# Sailing Fun

Read a story about Matt and his dad.

Matt and his dad enjoy sailing. When they sail, they like to listen to music. Matt likes fast, loud music. His dad likes slow, soft music. Matt and his dad have lunch on the boat, too. Matt likes hot dogs. His dad likes ham sandwiches.

Put an **X** in the box or boxes that answer each question.

Matt and his dad are alike. They both like

☐ sailing        ☐ music        ☐ hot dogs

Matt and his dad are different.

For lunch, Matt likes a

☐ ham sandwich      ☐ hot dog

For lunch, his dad likes a

☐ ham sandwich   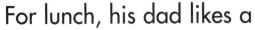   ☐ hot dog

Name _____

# What Happens Next

Draw a line to match the cause to the effect.

| **Cause** | **Effect** |
|---|---|

Name _____

# I Can Circle What Happens Next

Circle the picture that shows what will happen next.

Daniel threw a stick across the yard for his dog, Muffy.

Muffy will take a nap.

Muffy will run to get the stick.

Rachel wrote a letter. She put it in an envelope and put a stamp on it.

Rachel will put the letter in the mailbox.

Rachel will put the letter in the bathtub.

The cake was cool. Tyler got the bowl of frosting.

Tyler will cut the cake.

Tyler will frost the cake.

77

*Essential Skills and Practice Grade K*

Name _____

# One, Two, Buckle My Shoe

Say the nursery rhyme. Clap out the beat.
Make one clap on each **bold** word.

**One**, **two**,
**Buckle** my **shoe**.

**Three**, **four**,
**Shut** the **door**.

**Five**, **six**,
**Pick** up **sticks**.

**Seven**, **eight**,
**Lay** them **straight**.

**Nine**, **ten**,
A **big** fat **hen**.

Name _____

# Size Search

Cut out the animal cards below. Glue each animal under the correct size.

| small | medium | big |
|-------|--------|-----|
|       |        |     |
|       |        |     |
|       |        |     |

Name _____

# The Pick of the Garden

Circle the animal that is biggest in each row.

**Robin**

**Grasshopper**

**Beetle**

**Butterfly**

**Rabbit**

**Snail**

**Caterpillar**

**Hummingbird**

**Squirrel**

*Essential Skills and Practice Grade K*

Name _____

# Perfectly Pleasing Patterns

Circle the object that comes next.
Color the pictures.

*Essential Skills and Practice Grade K*

MATH

Name _____

# Grow a Garden

Circle the item that comes next in each row.

Name _____

# Animal Parade

Circle the animal that comes next in each parade.

   |

 |

  |

   |

*Essential Skills and Practice Grade K*

MATH

Name _____

# Drawing Shapes

Trace.　　Draw.

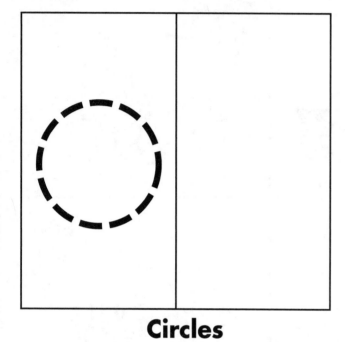

**Circles**

Trace.　　Draw.

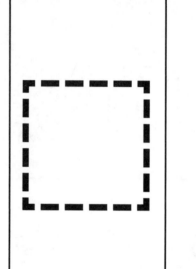

**Squares**

Trace.　　Draw.

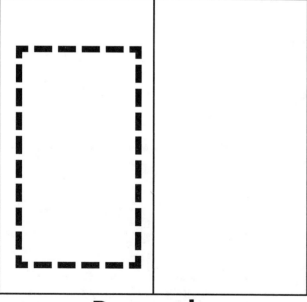

**Rectangles**

Trace.　　Draw.

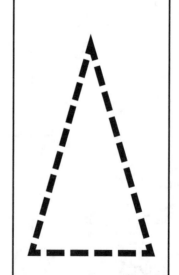

**Triangles**

Name _____

# Floating Up

Color **6** ◯ orange.

Color **7** ☆ blue.

85

Name _____

# Shape Words

Trace and say the shape word. Draw lines to match the shape word to the object.

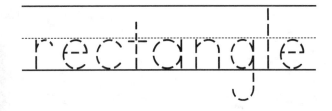

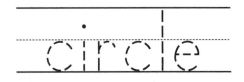

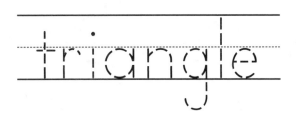

Name _____

# Other Shapes

Trace and draw.

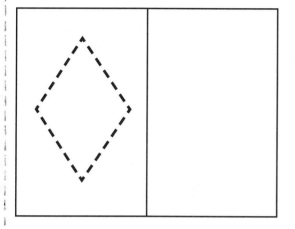

diamond

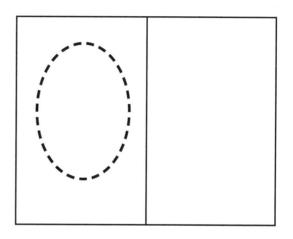

oval

heart

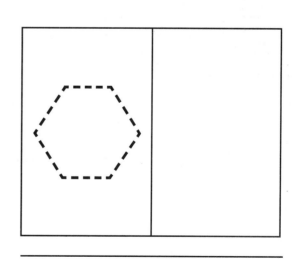

hexagon

87    *Essential Skills and Practice Grade K*

Name _____

# Fun on the Farm

Find the circles, triangles, and squares.
Color them. Color the rest of the picture.

*Essential Skills and Practice Grade K*

Name _____

# Matching Shapes

Look at each row. Say the shape name.
Color the objects that have the same shape.

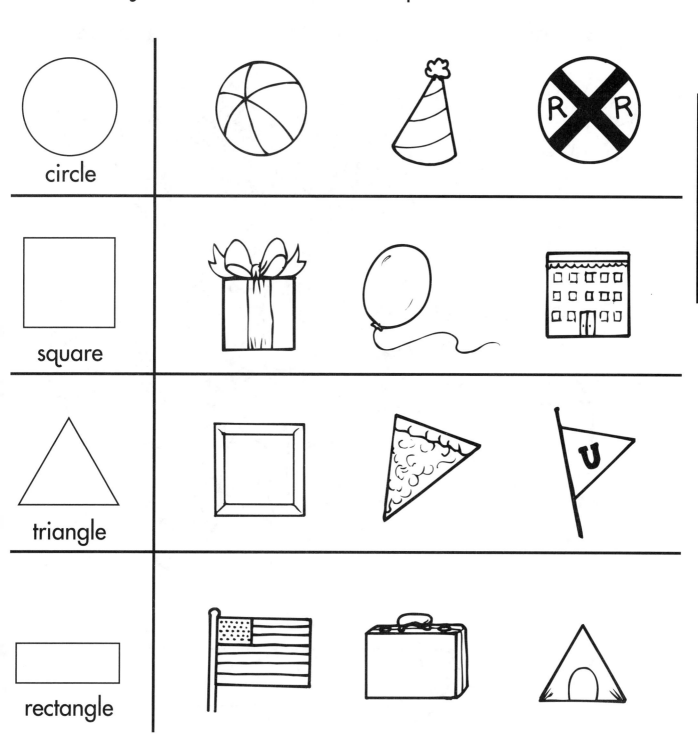

circle

square

triangle

rectangle

*Essential Skills and Practice Grade K*

Name _____

# A Blooming Success!

Color the flower blossoms.
Use the number key to help you.

**1 = pink**          **2 = blue**          **3 = purple**

*Essential Skills and Practice Grade K*

Name _____

# A Yummy Number

To find the mystery number, color the spaces with these numbers purple.

**9   5   8   7   10   13   18   17   20   19   11**

| 8 | 10 | 7 | 15 |
|---|----|---|----|
| 18 | 6 | 16 | 1 |
| 17 | 5 | 9 | 4 |
| 2 | 14 | 19 | 12 |
| 11 | 13 | 20 | 3 |

Circle the mystery number.    **5      10      18**

Name _____

# Water Wonder

Color to find the hidden picture.

**5** = yellow          **7** = green          **10** = blue

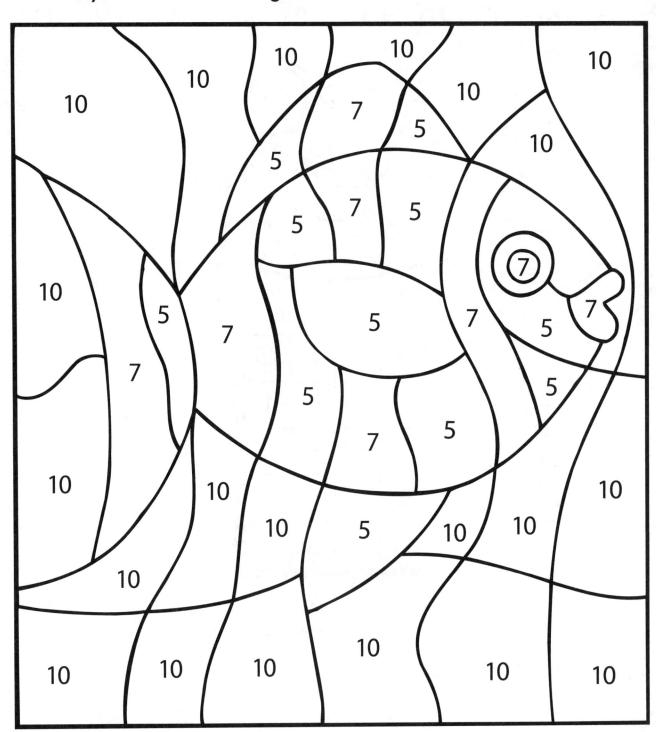

*Essential Skills and Practice Grade K*

Name _____

# Polly Want a Cracker?

Color to find the hidden picture.

**13** = green     **14** = orange     **15** = yellow

*Essential Skills and Practice Grade K*

Name _____

# Floating Away

Color to find the hidden picture.

**18** = blue     **19** = red     **20** = yellow

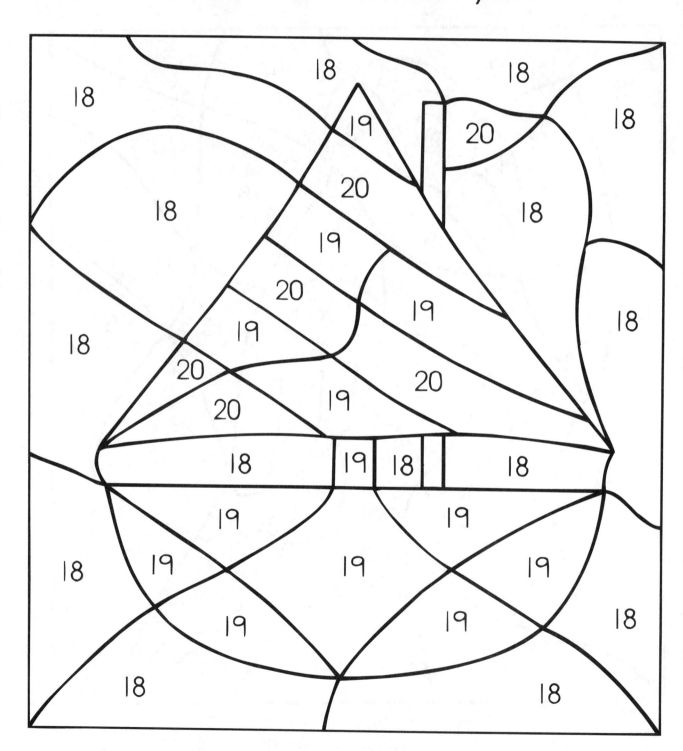

*Essential Skills and Practice Grade K*

Name _____

# Count and Write

Trace the numbers.

| | | | | |
|---|---|---|---|---|
| 1 | 2 | 3 | 4 | 5 |
| 6 | 7 | 8 | 9 | 10 |

Write the numbers from 1 to 10.

| | | | | |
|---|---|---|---|---|
| 1 | 2 | ___ | 4 | ___ |
| ___ | 7 | ___ | 9 | ___ |

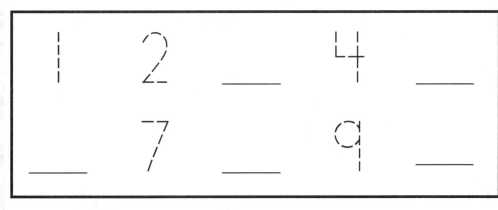

| | | | | |
|---|---|---|---|---|
| ___ | 2 | 3 | ___ | ___ |
| 6 | ___ | 8 | ___ | 10 |

*Essential Skills and Practice Grade K*

MATH

Name _____

# Let's Count

Write the missing numbers.

Name _____

# Number Connector

Connect the number words in order.
Then color the number you made.

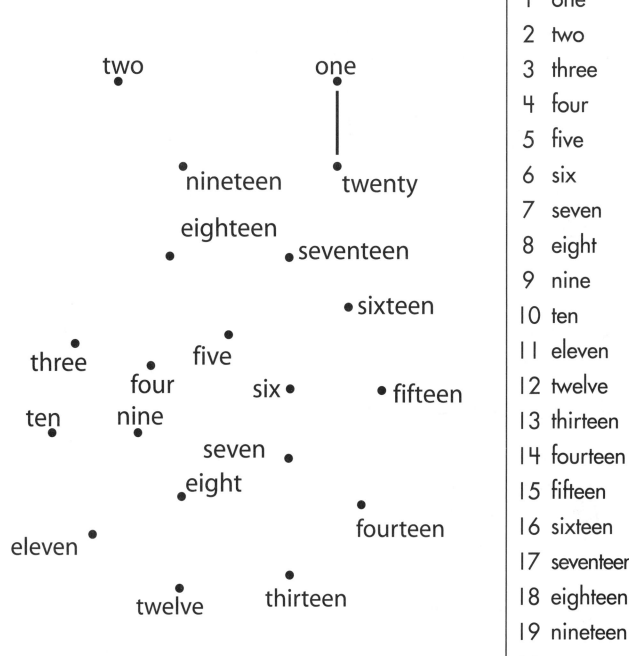

| | |
|---|---|
| 1 | one |
| 2 | two |
| 3 | three |
| 4 | four |
| 5 | five |
| 6 | six |
| 7 | seven |
| 8 | eight |
| 9 | nine |
| 10 | ten |
| 11 | eleven |
| 12 | twelve |
| 13 | thirteen |
| 14 | fourteen |
| 15 | fifteen |
| 16 | sixteen |
| 17 | seventeen |
| 18 | eighteen |
| 19 | nineteen |
| 20 | twenty |

MATH

*Essential Skills and Practice Grade K*

Name _____

# Count and Match

Count. Draw a line to the correct number word. Trace each number word.

seven

three

five

nine

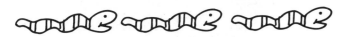

four

six

eight

*Essential Skills and Practice Grade K*

Name _____

# Counting Critters

Count the things in each group. Write the number word in the boxes by the pictures.

| 1 one | 2 two | 3 three | 4 four |
|-------|-------|---------|--------|
| 5 five | 6 six | 7 seven | 8 eight |
| 9 nine | 10 ten | 11 eleven | 12 twelve |

1.

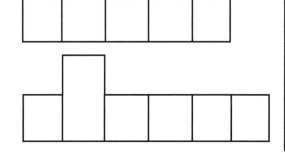

2.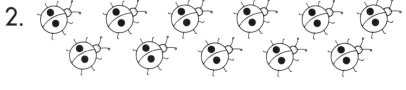

3.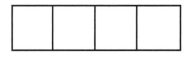

4.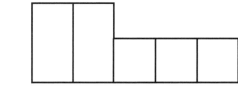

5.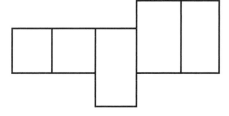

6.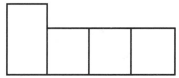

99

*Essential Skills and Practice Grade K*

Name _____

# Not a Dragon

Connect the dots from **1** to **12**. Color to finish the picture.

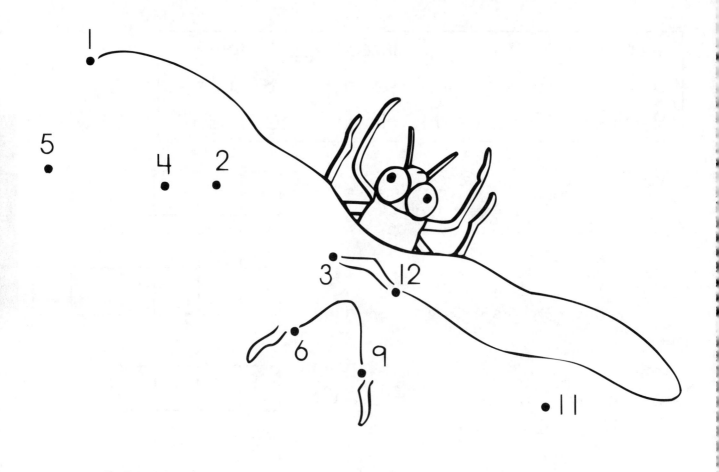

*Essential Skills and Practice Grade K*

Name _____

# Balancing Trick

Connect the dots from **1** to **20**. Color to finish the picture.

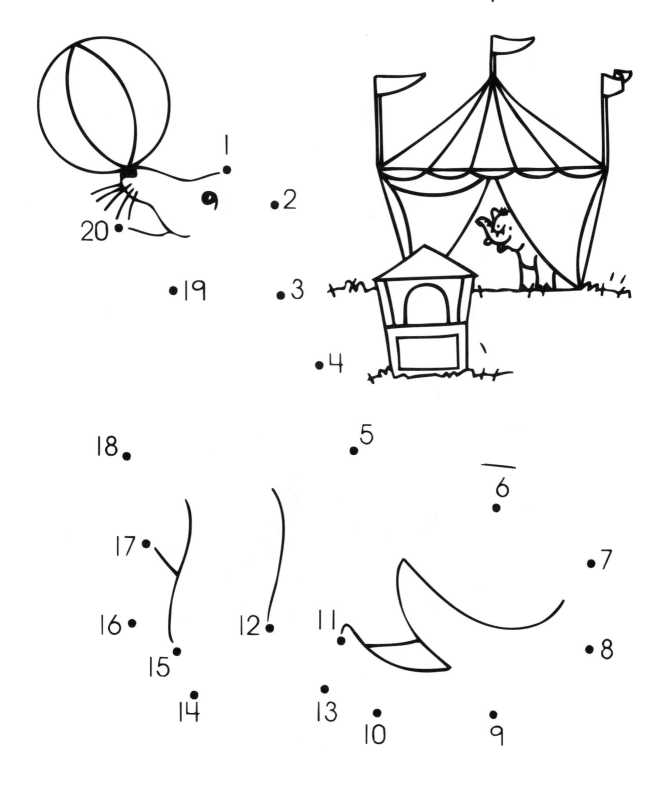

*Essential Skills and Practice Grade K*

Name _____

# In the Town Square

Connect the dots to see what is in the town square.

Name _____

# Making Music

Color the sets of 3.

**3**

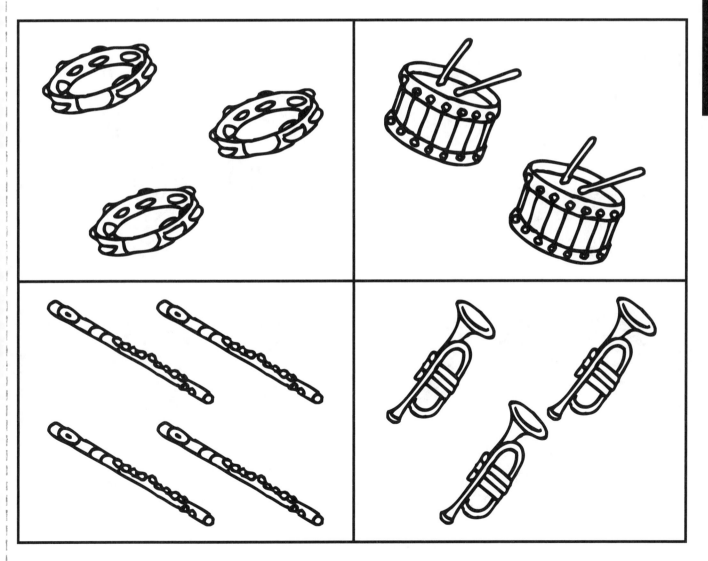

*Essential Skills and Practice Grade K*

Name _____

# Flower Power

Color the sets of 5.

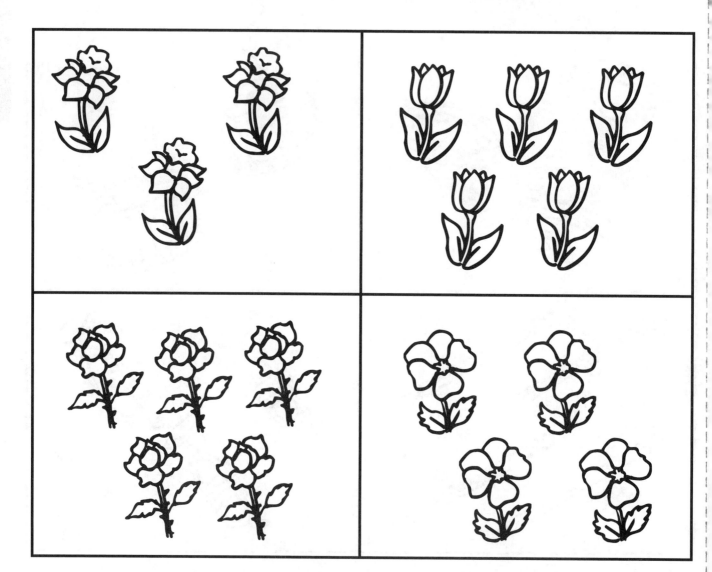

*Essential Skills and Practice Grade K*

Name _____

# Mouse Lunch

Find the food and color it green. Then color the rest of the picture.

Circle to show how many.

 **1  2  3**       **1  2**       **1  2  3**      🔺 **1  2  3**

*Essential Skills and Practice Grade K*

Name _____

# Farm Count

Count the objects. Write the number.

*Essential Skills and Practice Grade K*

Name _____

# Gardening Counting

Count the objects. Write the number.
Circle the smaller number.

*Essential Skills and Practice Grade K*

Name _____

# Barnyard Hoedown

Count the animals and trace the letters below. Color.

 seven      eight

 nine      ten

*Essential Skills and Practice Grade K*

Name _____

# Bird Buddies

Find the numbers **1** to **10** in the picture. Color them.

*Essential Skills and Practice Grade K*

MATH

Name _____

# I Can Count

Count and color.

Color 1.

Color 2.

Color 3.

Color 4.

Color 5.

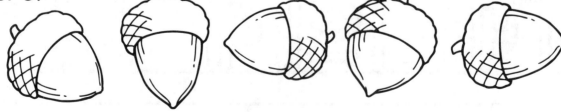

*Essential Skills and Practice Grade K*

Name _____

# It's a Ten

Draw more objects to make ten in each set. Then color the pictures.

1.

2.

3.

4.

5.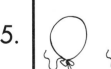

*Essential Skills and Practice Grade K*

Name _____

# Tally It Up

Use tally marks to show how many objects are in each box.

| I | I I | I I I | I I I I | ⊥⊥⊥ | ⊥⊥⊥ I |
|---|-----|-------|---------|-----|-------|
| 1 | 2 | 3 | 4 | 5 | 6 |

*Essential Skills and Practice Grade K*

Name _____

# Count the Objects

Count. Circle the number.

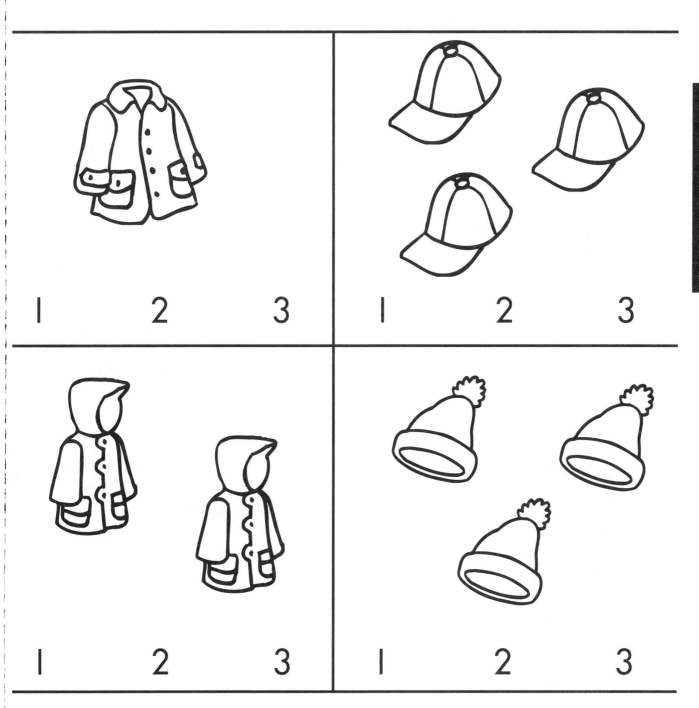

Name _____

# Animals in Winter

## Count the animals. Circle the matching number.

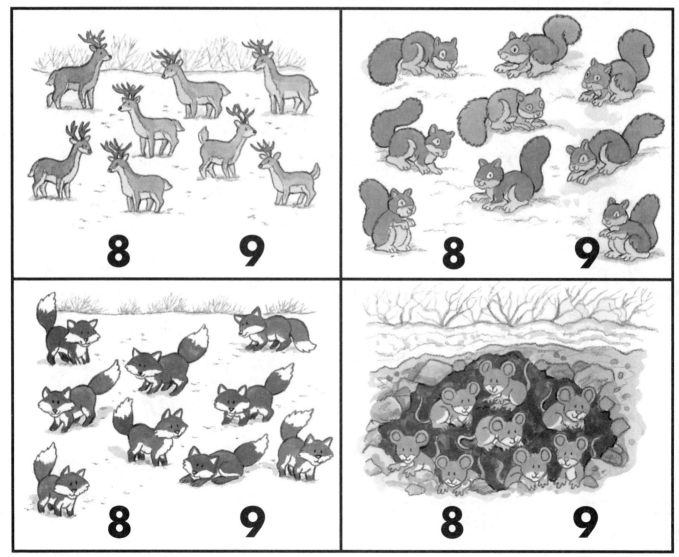

*Essential Skills and Practice Grade K*

Name _____

# Super Circles

Count the circles. Color them.

Circle to show how many circles you found.

**11    12    13    14    15    16    17    18    19    20**

*Essential Skills and Practice Grade K*

Name _____

# Spotty Leopards

Circle the number of spots on each leopard.

*Essential Skills and Practice Grade K*

Name _____

# I Can Write Numbers
Trace. Count and circle the pictures.

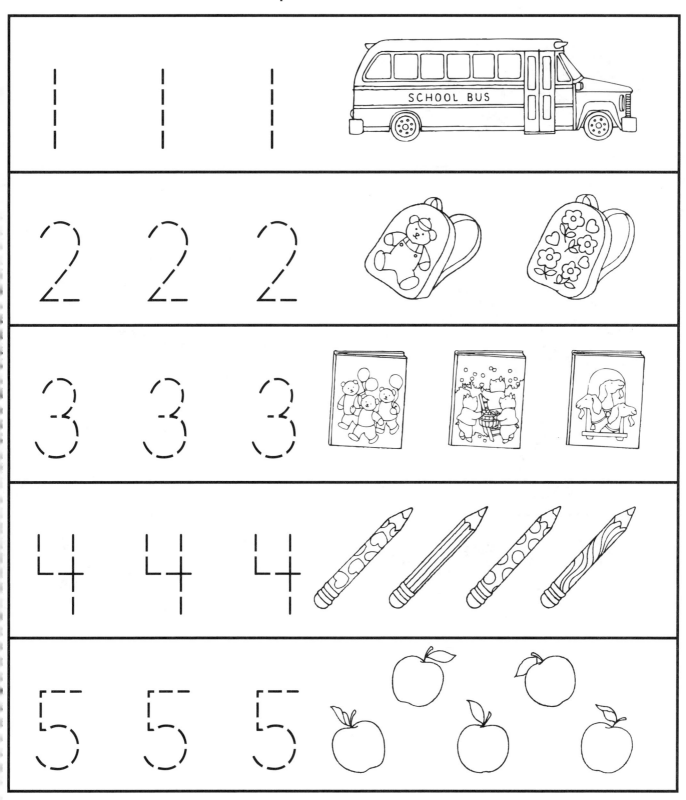

*Essential Skills and Practice Grade K*

Name _____

# Clean and Healthy

Trace the number that tells how many.

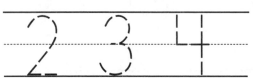

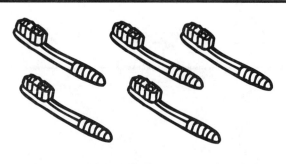

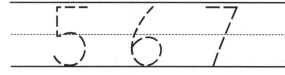

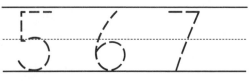

118

Name _____

# Elephant Snacks

Count the peanuts in each bag.
Then write the number on the line.

Name _____

# Stringing Numbers

On each string, draw enough beads to show the number.

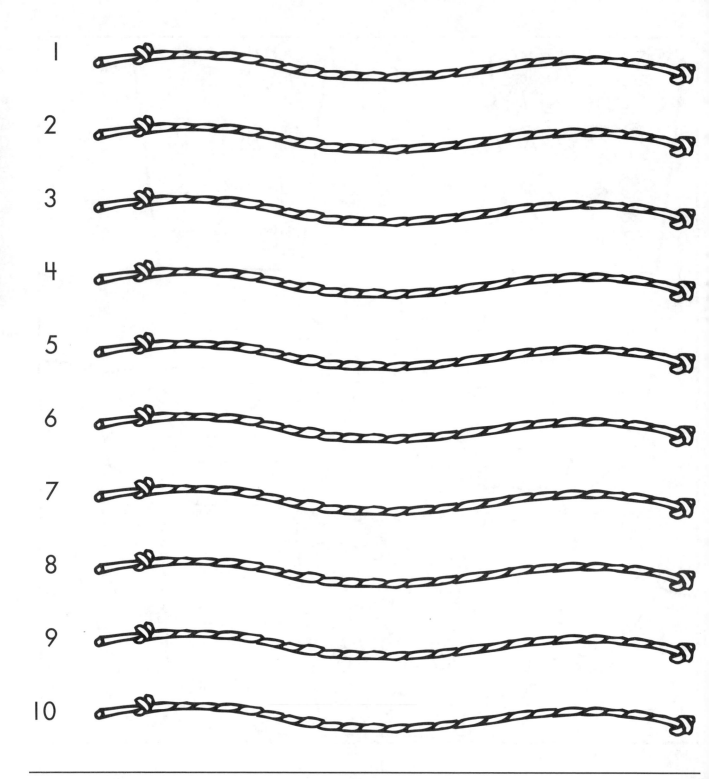

Name _____

# Mouse Hunt

Find **10** mice below. Color them.
Color the rest of the picture.

*Essential Skills and Practice Grade K*

Name _____

# Nut Hunt

Find the nuts . Color them brown. Then color the rest of the picture. Can you find **II** nuts in all?

*Essential Skills and Practice Grade K*

Name _____

# Big Jumpers!

Find the grasshoppers . Color them green. Then color the rest of the picture. Can you find **12** grasshoppers in all?

*Essential Skills and Practice Grade K*

MATH

Name _____

# Monkeying Around

Find the bananas . Color them yellow. Then color the rest of the picture. Can you find **15** bananas in all?

*Essential Skills and Practice Grade K*

Name _____

# Color Creations

Find the crayons . Color them purple. Then color the rest of the picture. Can you find **18** crayons in all?

*Essential Skills and Practice Grade K*

Name _____

# Feeding the Birds

Draw **15** more pieces of birdseed in the bag.
Then answer the question below.

How many pieces of birdseed are in the bag now? _____

*Essential Skills and Practice Grade K*

Name _____

# Clever Clover

Look carefully at the picture. Find the **25** hidden shamrocks. Color them green.

*Essential Skills and Practice Grade K*

Name _____

# Fish Bowl

Color **20** fish.

Circle to show how many fish are left over.     **5**     **6**     **7**

*Essential Skills and Practice Grade K*

Name _____

# Snail Garden

Color **25** snails brown  .

Circle to show how many snails are left over.    **3**    **4**    **5**

*Essential Skills and Practice Grade K*

Name _____

# Piggy Bank

Color **24** pennies brown .

Circle to show how many pennies are left over.   **2**   **3**   **4**

*Essential Skills and Practice Grade K*

Name _____

# Which Is More?

Count the objects in each group. For each row, circle the group with the larger number. Then color the objects.

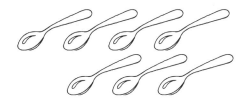 OR

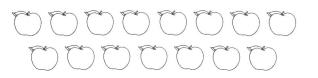 OR

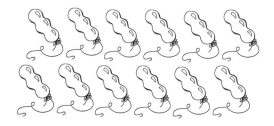 OR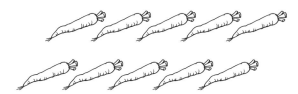

 OR

 OR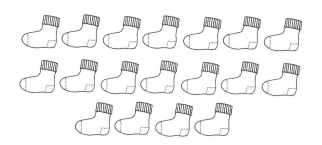

MATH

*Essential Skills and Practice Grade K*

Name _____

# Finding Friends

Help Tommy Turtle find his friends.
Color the path that goes in order
from **1** to **8**.

Name _____

# I Can Play

Draw a path to each toy by counting from 1 to 9.

Name _____

# Ready to Land

Count from **1** to **20** to take the plane to the hangar.

*Essential Skills and Practice Grade K*

Name _____

# A–mazing Football

Get Freddy Football to the end zone by counting by 2s.
Starting with 2, color the footballs that contain numbers counting
by 2 until you reach the end zone and score a touchdown.

Name _____

# Crazy Counting

Trace. Write the missing numbers.

Count by twos.

2 ___ ___ 6 8 ___

Count by fives.

  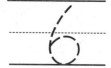 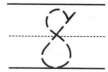 

5 10 ___ 20 ___

Count by tens.

10 ___ 30 ___ 50

*Essential Skills and Practice Grade K*

Name _____

# Add them Up

Write the numbers that tell how many.

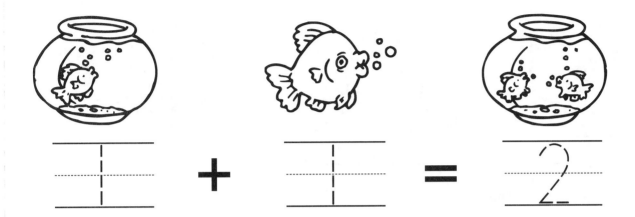

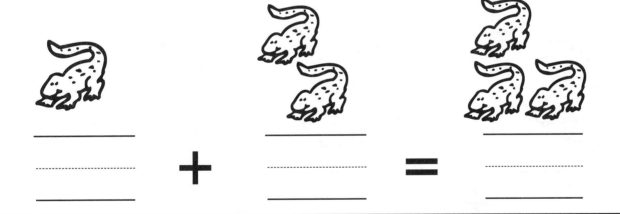

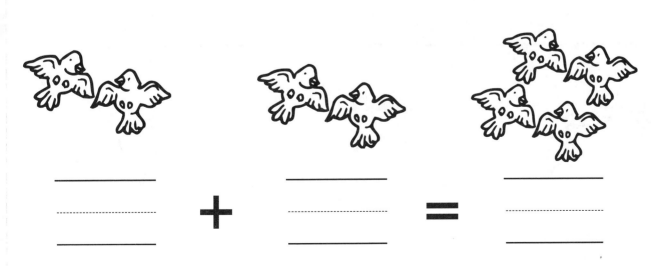

*Essential Skills and Practice Grade K*

MATH

Name _____

# How Many in All?

Write the numbers that tell how many.

 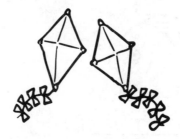 

 + 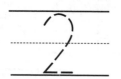 =

2 + 2 = 4

 +  = _____

_____ + _____ = _____

*Essential Skills and Practice Grade K*

Name _____

# A Special Friend

Add. Then color to find a special friend.

**3 = green**  **4 = blue**  **5 = brown**

*Essential Skills and Practice Grade K*

Name _____

# Add 'Em Up

Add the numbers.

2      +      3      = _____

1      +      6      = _____

4      +      4      = _____

2      +      4      = _____

5      +      2      = _____

*Essential Skills and Practice Grade K*

Name _____

# Starry Sums

Add the stars in each row. Write the sum on the line.

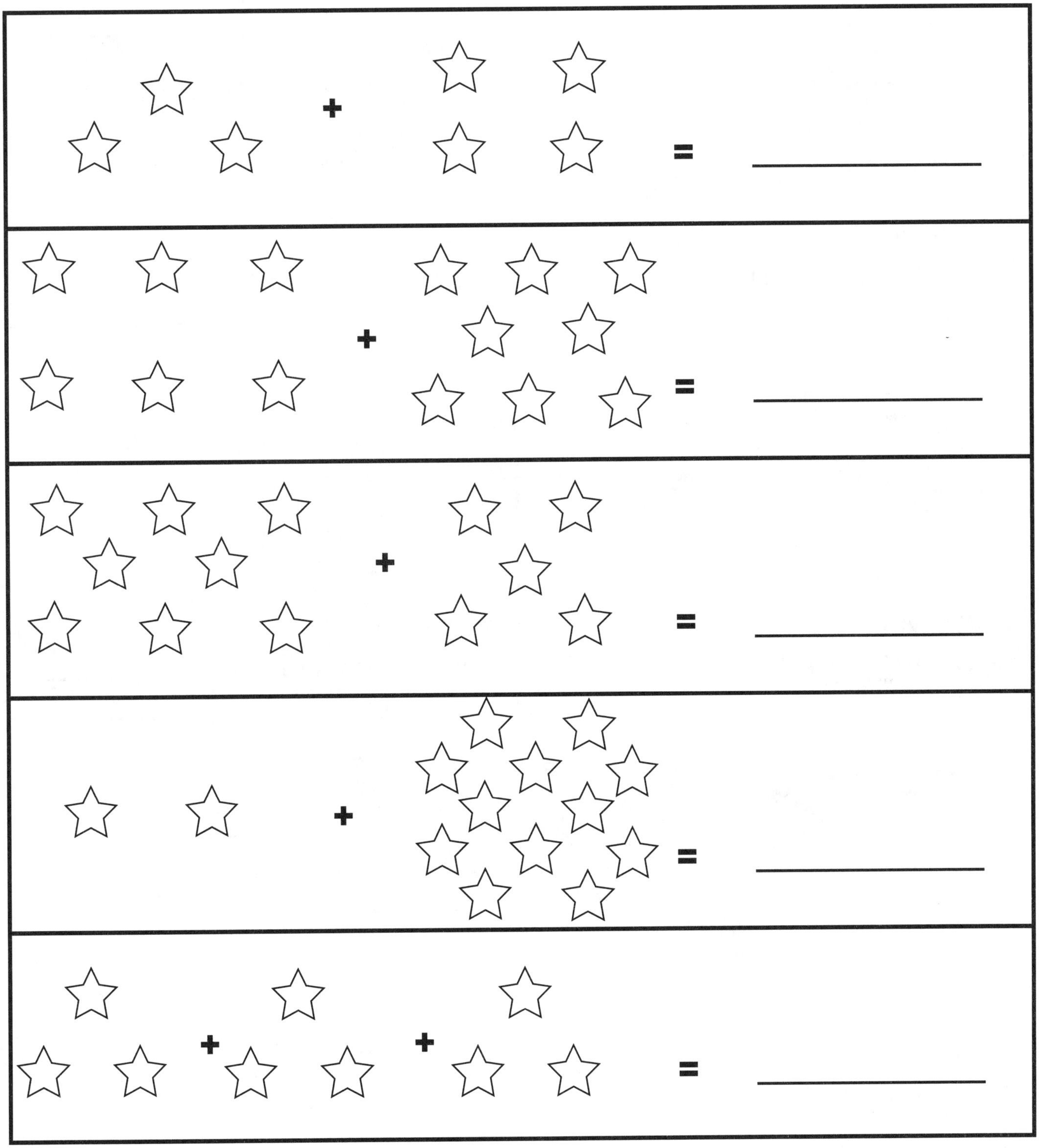

= _____

+ ... = _____

+ ... = _____

+ ... = _____

+ ... + ... = _____

141

Name _____

# In the Garden

Cross out 1.
How many are left? _____

Cross out 3.
How many are left? _____

Cross out 1.
How many are left? _____

Cross out 2.
How many are left? _____

Cross out 2.
How many are left? _____

Cross out 2.
How many are left? _____

Name _____

# Where Did They Go?

Any animal that has been crossed out is gone. How many
animals are left? Circle the number.

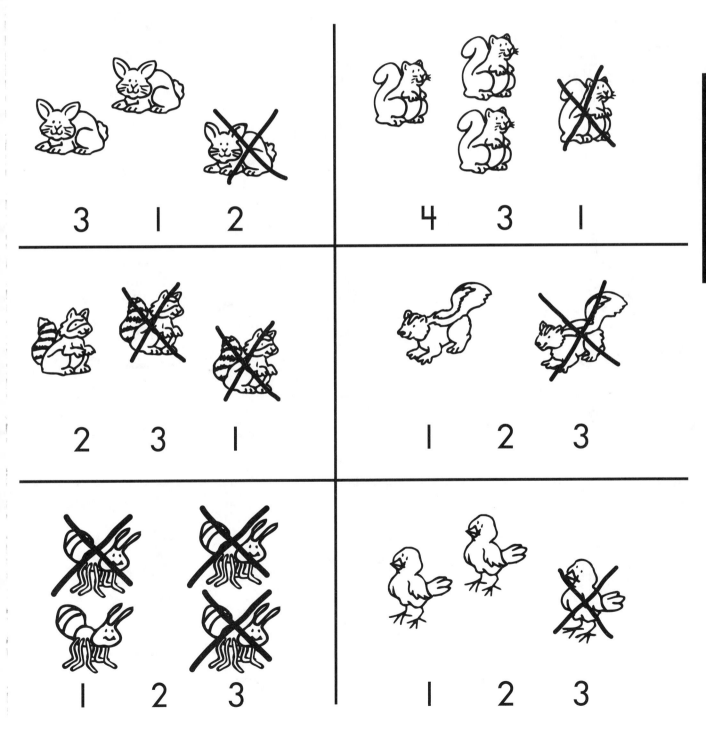

*Essential Skills and Practice Grade K*

MATH

Name _____

# How Many Are Left?

Write the numbers that tell how many.

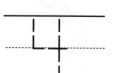 —  =

4 - 2 = 2

_____ — _____ = _____

_____ — _____ = _____

*Essential Skills and Practice Grade K*

Name _____

# Wholes and Halves

Look at the vegetables at the bottom of the page. Draw two halves next to the matching whole vegetable.

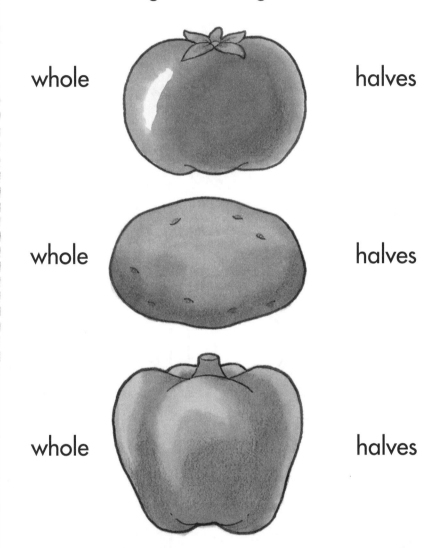

whole                                  halves

whole                                    halves

whole                                    halves

145                      *Essential Skills and Practice Grade K*

Name _____

# Half and Half

Look at the pictures below. Make each object whole by drawing its other half.

1.

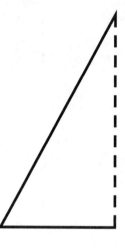

2.

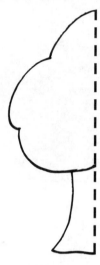

3.

4.

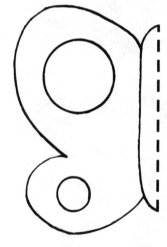

5.

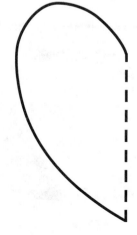

6.

*Essential Skills and Practice Grade K*

Name _____

# Where's the Turtle?

Write the place of the turtle.

**first**     **second**     **third**     **fourth**     **fifth**

first     second     _____     fourth     fifth

first     second     third     fourth     _____

first     _____     third     fourth     fifth

*Essential Skills and Practice Grade K*

MATH

Name _____

# Friends Go Hiking

The friends are following their leader on the trail.
Draw a line from each number-order word to the matching hiker.

**fourth**    **third**    **first**    **second**    **eighth**    **fifth**    **seventh**    **sixth**

*Essential Skills and Practice Grade K*

Name _____

# Money Mania

Add the coin values in each row. Write the total amount
on the line.

| penny<br>1¢ | nickel<br>5¢ | dime<br>10¢ | quarter<br>25¢ |
| --- | --- | --- | --- |

1. = _____

2. = _____

3. = _____

4. = _____

5. = _____

6. = _____

7. = _____

8. = _____

9. = _____

10. = _____

149                                    *Essential Skills and Practice Grade K*

Name _____

# Money Matters

Add the coin values in each row. Write the total amount on the line.

| penny 1¢ | nickel 5¢ | dime 10¢ | quarter 25¢ |
|---|---|---|---|

1.  = _____

2.   = _____

3.       = _____

4.     = _____

5.   = _____

6.   = _____

7.    = _____

8.    = _____

9.   = _____

10.   = _____

*Essential Skills and Practice Grade K*

Name _____

# What's Long?

Color the two in each set that are the same length.

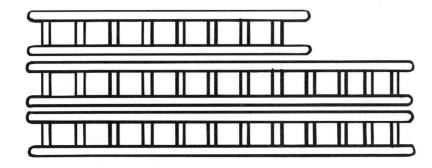

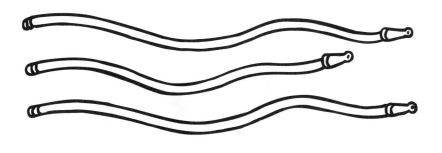

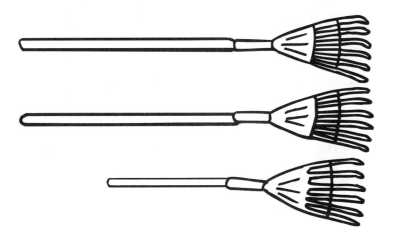

151  *Essential Skills and Practice Grade K*

Name _____

# Dinosaur Rule!

Scientists use rulers to measure dinosaur bones.
Write the missing numbers on the rulers.

1 ____ 3 ____ ____ 6

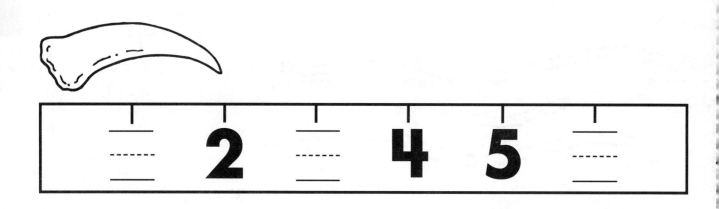

____ 2 ____ 4 5 ____

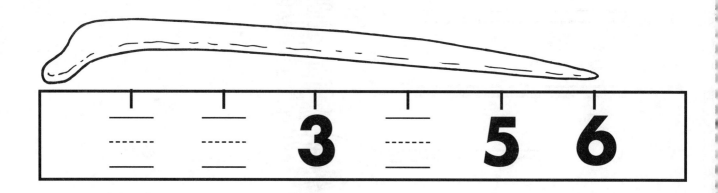

____ ____ 3 ____ 5 6

*Essential Skills and Practice Grade K*

Name _____

# I Can Measure

Draw a line from each child to the correct measuring tool.

What does Dan need to measure the sugar?

What does Jen need to weigh the oranges?

What does Jill need to measure how long the ribbon is?

What does Matt need to find out how cold it is?

MATH

Name _____

# Animal Graphs

Write how many. Circle the animal that has the most.
Color the animal that has the least.

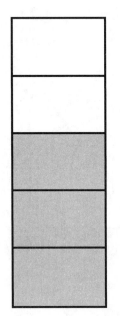 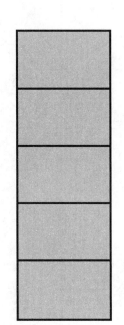 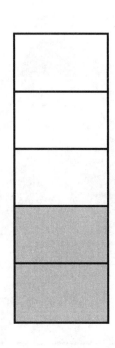

_____  _____  _____

- - - - - - - - - - - - -    - - - - - - - - - - - - -    - - - - - - - - - - - - -

_____  _____  _____

*Essential Skills and Practice Grade K*

Name _____

# Funny Frogs

Count the frogs and write the number.
Color a square for each frog.

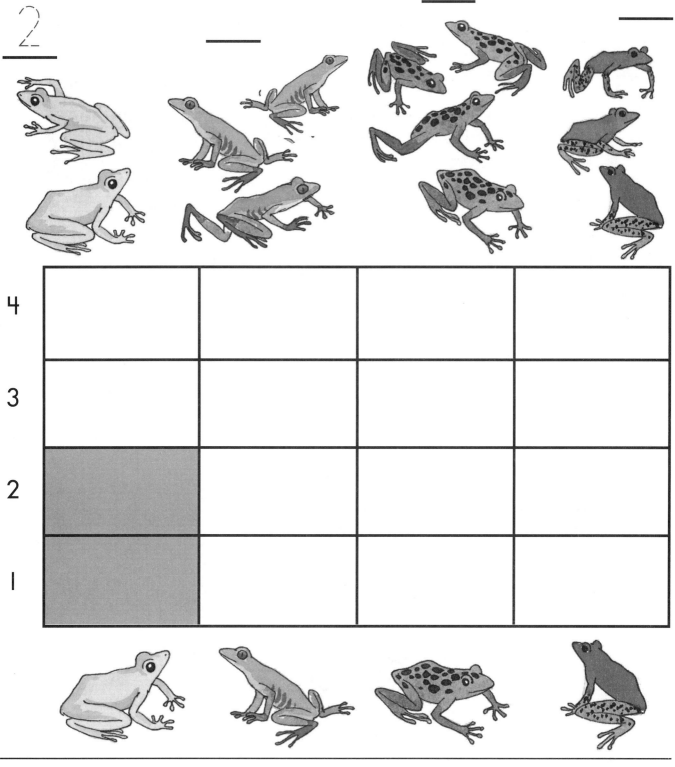

*Essential Skills and Practice Grade K*

Name _____

# Days of the Week

Trace the words. Say them.

The first day of the week.

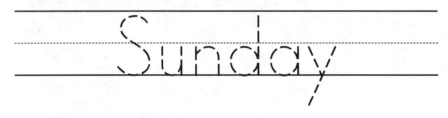

The second day of the week.

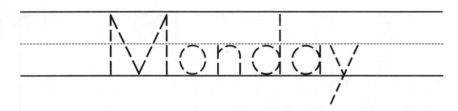

The third day of the week.

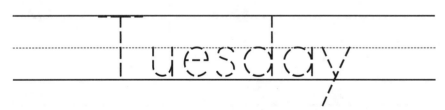

The fourth day of the week.

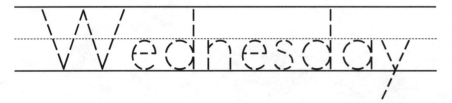

*Essential Skills and Practice Grade K*

Name _____

# More Days of the Week

Trace the words. Say them.

The fifth day of the week.

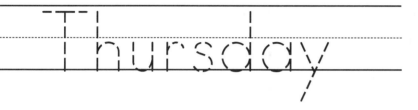

The sixth day of the week.

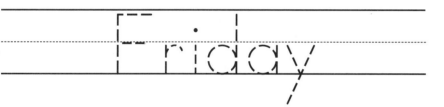

The seventh day of the week.

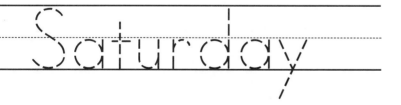

What's your favorite day of the week?

_____

_____

*Essential Skills and Practice Grade K*

# Time of Day

Trace and color. Draw a picture of something you do during each time of the day.

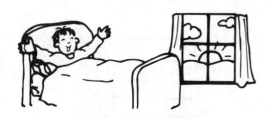

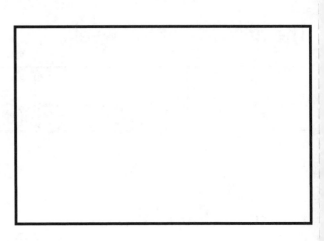

morning

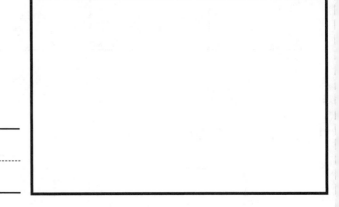

afternoon

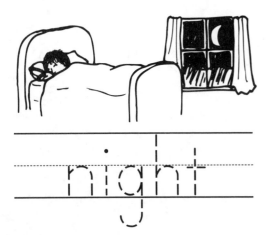

night

Name _____

# Body Parts

Point to the body parts. Say the name of each.
Trace the words.

head

arm

hand

leg

foot

*Essential Skills and Practice Grade K*

SCIENCE

Name _____

# Left and Right

Draw a ring on the right hand.
Draw a watch on the left wrist.

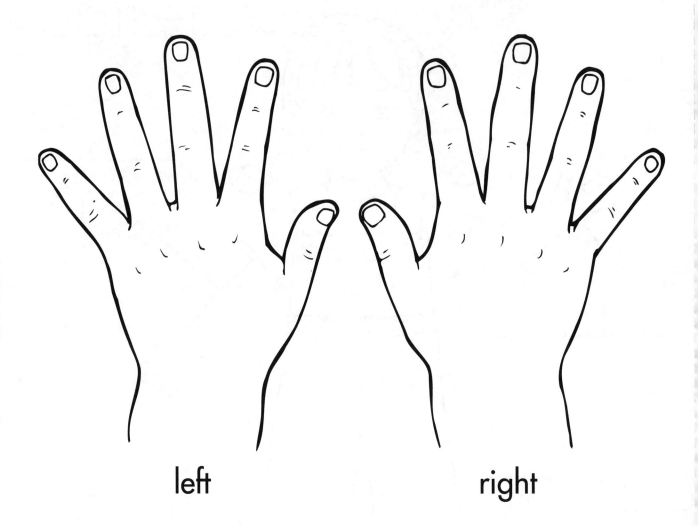

left                              right

When you draw or write, which hand do you use?

_____

---------------------------------

_____

Name _____

# My Hair

Draw a picture of your face and hair.

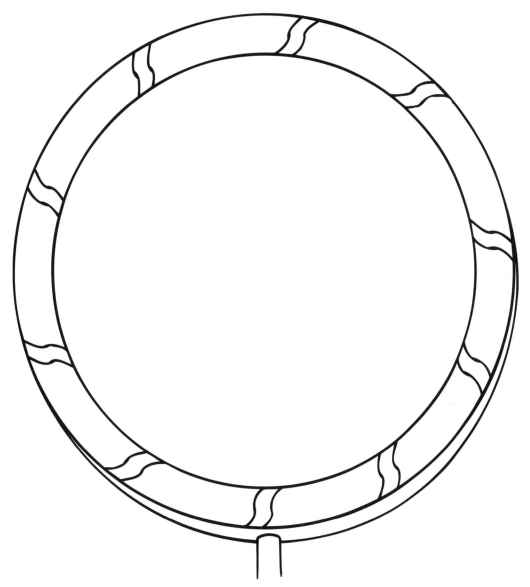

Circle.

My hair is _____.

**straight    curly    wavy**

The color is _____.

**brown    black    red    blond**

SCIENCE

Name _____

# My Feet

Draw a picture of your feet.

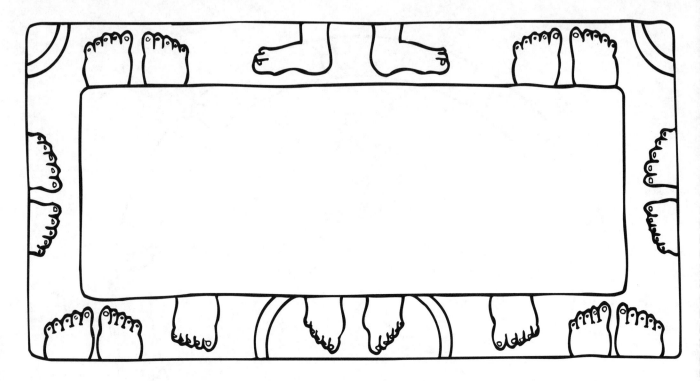

Color the things that your feet help you do.

162                    *Essential Skills and Practice Grade K*

Name _____

# My Five Senses

Which parts of the body help you see, hear, smell, taste, and touch?
Draw lines to show your answers.

I see with my

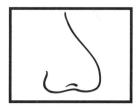

I hear with my

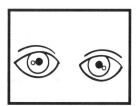

I smell with my

I taste with my

I touch with my

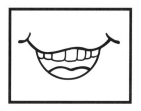

Name _____

# My Eyes

Draw a picture of your eyes.

Color the things you like to see.

*Essential Skills and Practice Grade K*

Name _____

# My Ears

Draw a picture of your ears.

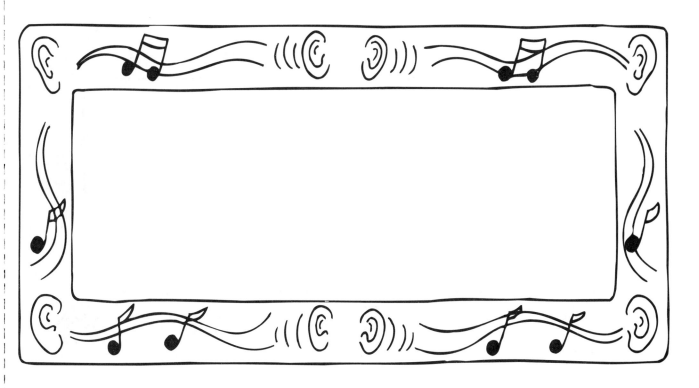

Color the things you like to hear.

SCIENCE

Name _____

# My Mouth

Draw a picture of your mouth and teeth.

Color the things you like to eat.

Name _____

# My Hands

Draw a picture of your hands.

Color the things you like to touch.

*Essential Skills and Practice Grade K*

SCIENCE

# I Brush My Teeth

Circle the things that you use to brush your teeth.

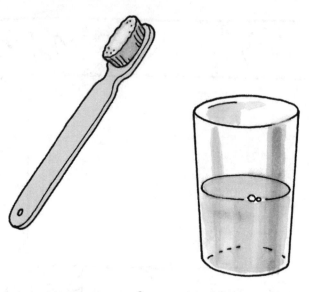

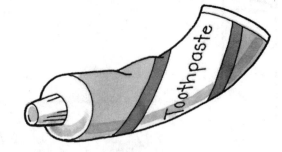

Draw a picture of yourself
brushing your teeth.

Brush your teeth,
Clean and floss,
Show those cavities
Who's the boss!

*Essential Skills and Practice Grade K*

Name _____

# I Am Growing

_____
.............................
I weigh _____ pounds.

_____
.............................
I am _____ inches tall.

Color the things that help you grow.

SCIENCE

Name _____

# I Eat Healthful Snacks

Circle six healthful snacks.

*Essential Skills and Practice Grade K*

Name _____

# Healthy Hang-Ups

Create a mobile using the pieces below. Color these foods and cut out. Punch holes at the top of each piece and hang from a clothes hanger or dowel.

*Essential Skills and Practice Grade K*

Name _____

# Let's Eat Dinner!

Read each sentence. Draw a line to the matching picture.

I will eat spaghetti.

I will eat green beans.

I will eat bread.

I will eat a cupcake.

*Essential Skills and Practice Grade K*

SCIENCE

Name _____

# My Favorite Food

Finish the sentence. Draw a picture to match.

My favorite dinner meal

is _____

My favorite drink is _____

_____

Here is what I like to eat for dinner.

*Essential Skills and Practice Grade K*

Name _____

# Plant at Work

Cut out the pictures. Match and paste them in order.

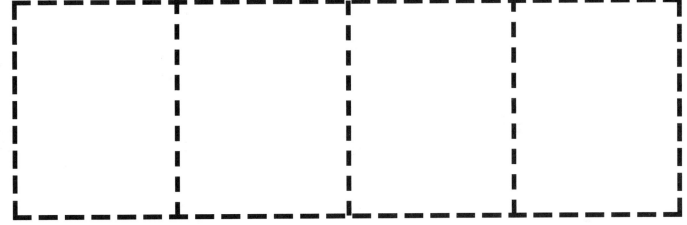

The seed is planted in soil.

A root grows down into the soil.

The stem pushes up toward the sun.

The stem grows and leaves unfold.

SCIENCE

plants

Name _____

# Plant Fun

Find the word in each row. Color the boxes to show
the word.

seed

root

stem

dirt

sun

water

leaf

| s | e | e | d | x |
| b | r | o | o | t |
| s | t | e | m | p |
| d | i | r | t | l |
| a | s | u | n | k |
| w | a | t | e | r |
| t | l | e | a | f |

SCIENCE

177          *Essential Skills and Practice Grade K*

Name _____

# Parts of a Plant

Trace the words and the lines. Color the plant.

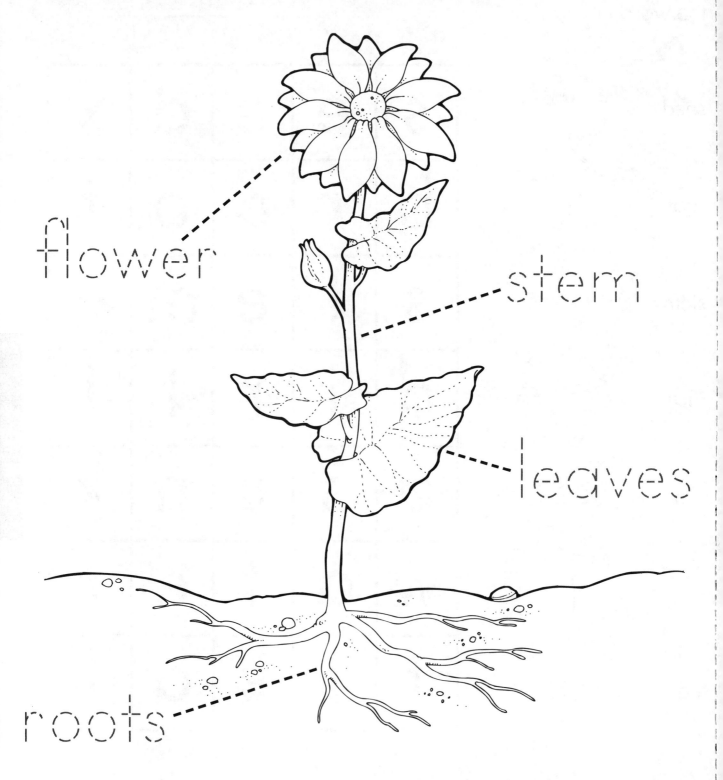

Name _____

# Eating Plants

Trace the words.

## We Eat Parts of Plants

corn

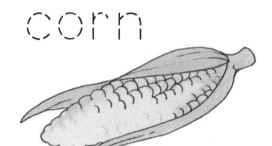

We eat seeds.

carrots

We eat roots.

celery

We eat stems.

lettuce

We eat leaves.

apples

We eat fruits.

*Essential Skills and Practice Grade K*

SCIENCE

Name _____

# At the Market

Look at the picture. Find **3** foods. Write their names.

oranges

toys

mom

baby

cereal

apples

cart

1. _____

2. _____

3. _____

Name _____

# Plants We Eat

Circle the words. The words go → and ↓.

| k | p | u | m | p | k | i | n | l |
|---|---|---|---|---|---|---|---|---|
| c | i | f | n | u | c | l | a | e |
| e | f | s | c | a | r | r | o | t |
| l | y | b | r | g | d | q | d | t |
| e | m | p | c | o | r | n | w | u |
| r | o | v | z | m | v | j | h | c |
| y | e | b | e | a | n | s | r | e |

 carrot

 corn

 lettuce

 pumpkin

 celery

 beans

SCIENCE

Name _____

# Plant Groups

Cross out the plant in each box that does not belong. Color the other plants.

*Essential Skills and Practice Grade K*

Name _____

# Trees Give Many Gifts

Circle the pictures that show ways people use trees and things that come from trees.

SCIENCE

*Essential Skills and Practice Grade K*

Name _____

# A Special Garden

Draw a picture of yourself standing in a garden.

Describe what you see standing in the garden.

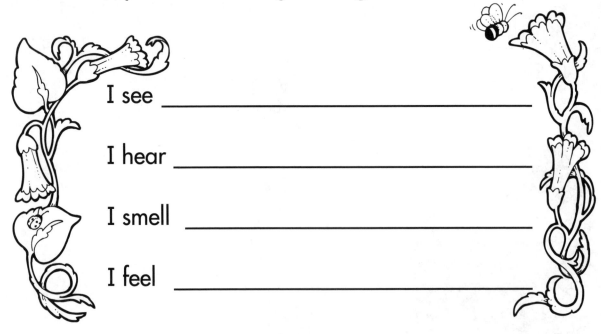

I see _____

I hear _____

I smell _____

I feel _____

Name _____

# Garden Days

Circle and write the best title for each picture.

A Long Nap

No More Weeds

Smell the Flowers

_____

- - - - - - - - - - - - - - - - - - - - - - - - -

_____

A Sweet Lunch

A Big Bird

Trees Are Green

_____

- - - - - - - - - - - - - - - - - - - - - - - - -

_____

*Essential Skills and Practice Grade K*

Name _____

# Out of Place

Circle **1** thing in each box that does not belong.
Answer the question at the bottom.

Everything circled is a kind of what? _____

Name _____

# In the Forest

Look at the picture. Find **3** living things.
Write their names.

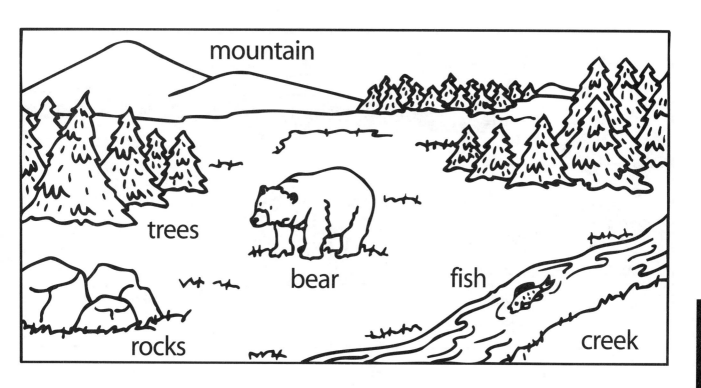

trees

mountain

bear

fish

rocks

creek

1. _____

2. _____

3. _____

*Essential Skills and Practice Grade K*

Name _____

# At the Farm

Look at the picture. Find **3** living things.
Write their names.

1. _____

2. _____

3. _____

Name _____

# Pets We Like

Color the pictures. Say the words. Check off the pets you have or would like to have.

☐ turtle

☐ bird

☐ snake

☐ dog

☐ cat

☐ rabbit

Name _____

# How Animals Move

Tell how each animal moves. Trace the words.

swims

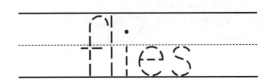

flies

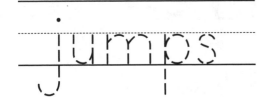

jumps

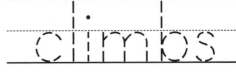

climbs

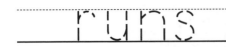

runs

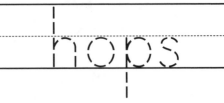

hops

*Essential Skills and Practice Grade K*

Name _____

# Flying High

Color the things that fly.

Name _____

# I Want My Mommy!

Trace the line from each baby to its mother.

Name _____

# Little Lost Lamb

Help the lamb find its mother.

*Essential Skills and Practice Grade K*

SCIENCE

Name _____

# Mrs. Cow's Friends

Trace the names of Mrs. Cow's barnyard friends. Color.

1. horse

2. piglets

3. rooster

4. lamb

5. dog

6. mouse

7. cat

*Essential Skills and Practice Grade K*

Name _____

# Search and Find

Find the objects in the woods. Color them.

 deer     eggs     squirrel     fish     frog     snake

SCIENCE

*Essential Skills and Practice Grade K*

Name _____

# A Beaver Family

Help the beavers get out of their house.

*Essential Skills and Practice Grade K*

Name _____

# The Zoo

Finish each sentence with the name of an animal.

**bear**

**monkey**

**snake**

**zebra**

I see a _____ .

I see a _____ .

I see a _____ .

I see a _____ .

*Essential Skills and Practice Grade K*

SCIENCE

Name _____

# Hear Me Roar!

Connect the dots from 1 to 10. Color.

Name _____

# Where Are the Tigers?

Help the boy find his way to the tigers.

*Essential Skills and Practice Grade K*

Name _____

# Zoo Puppets

You can create paper bag puppets to look like your favorite zoo animals. Just follow these simple directions.

Get a paper bag that fits easily over your hand. You will make your head on the end of your paper bag. The side with the fold will be the front of your animal's head. Draw or paste on your animal's eyes and nose. Don't forget to add ears on the back of the head.

Put your hand inside the paper bag and move the fold up and down with your hand. This part of the bag will be the mouth. Draw or paste on teeth and a tongue.

Decorate the front of the bag to look like the body of your animal. Add a tail if you need to!

Name _____

# Train Safari

Help the train take the right path through the forest. Watch out for elephants!

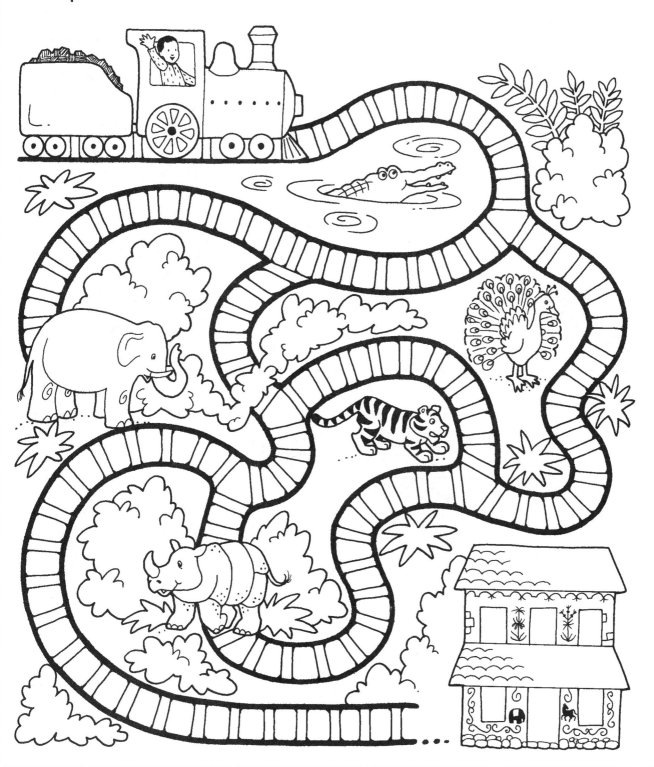

*Essential Skills and Practice Grade K*

Name _____

# Rain Forest Animals

Look at the picture. Read the words. Write the words on the lines.

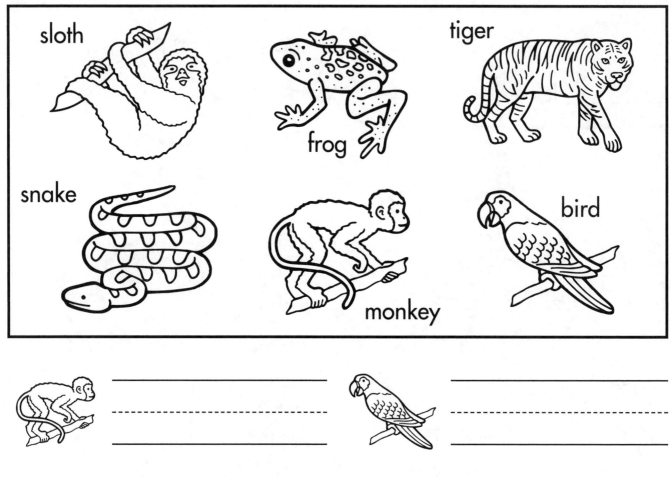

 _____

 _____

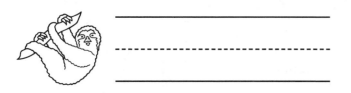 _____

 _____

*Essential Skills and Practice Grade K*

Name _____

# A Warm, Wet Forest

A rain forest is warm. Rain falls most days.
The rain forest is always green.

Color the trees and plants green.
Then draw falling rain. Color
the animals.

*Essential Skills and Practice Grade K*

Name _____

# What's Wrong?

In each picture, cross out the part that cannot really happen. Color the pictures.

*Essential Skills and Practice Grade K*

Name _____

# Ocean Home

Color the pictures. Read about ocean habitats.

Some animals live near the shore of the ocean.

Some animals live in very deep ocean waters.

Some animals live near the top of the ocean waters.

Some animals fly above the ocean waters.

SCIENCE

Name _____

# Ocean Animals

Write each animal's name in the correct place.

| Whale | shark |
|-------|-------|
| crab  | clam  |
| gull  | fish  |

*Essential Skills and Practice Grade K*

Name _____

# Fishy Friends

Help the striped fish swim through the coral and find its friend.

*Essential Skills and Practice Grade K*

Name _____

# Beautiful Birds

Circle the words. The words go → and ↓.

| s | g | p | m | e | b | r | e | t |
|---|---|---|---|---|---|---|---|---|
| p | c | a | r | d | i | n | a | l |
| a | r | r | d | o | r | o | g | c |
| r | n | r | a | s | t | u | l | h |
| r | i | o | w | o | w | l | e | m |
| o | x | t | l | y | k | f | p | l |
| w | d | v | f | r | o | b | i | n |

 sparrow

 cardinal

 parrot

 owl

 robin

 eagle

*Essential Skills and Practice Grade K*

Name _____

# Spiders

Color. Read about spiders.

Spiders are not insects.
Insects have six legs.
Spiders have eight legs.

Spiders spin sticky webs
to make homes and
to catch food.

Insects get stuck in
the webs. The spiders
spin silk around the insects
and eat them for dinner!

SCIENCE

Name _____

# A Bunch of Butterflies

Color the butterfly that is different.

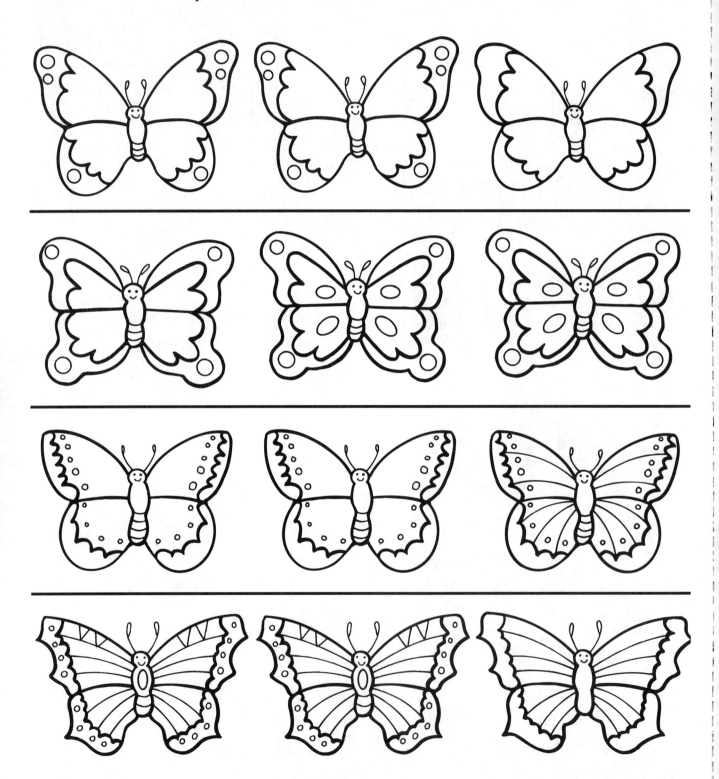

*Essential Skills and Practice Grade K*

Name _____

# Go Buggy!

Unscramble each word. Use the Word Bank for help. Write the words in the puzzle.

**Word Bank**

wasp

moth

bee

ant

grasshopper

mosquito

butterfly

cricket

## Down

1. rkctice
2. ebe
3. omht

## Across

4. paws
5. ytebrutlf
6. oqistomu
7. psogsrphaer
8. tna

SCIENCE

Name _____

# Bug Walk

Show the bug how to cross the leaf.

*Essential Skills and Practice Grade K*

Name _____

# A Bunch of Beetles

Find the **3** beetles that match. Color them.

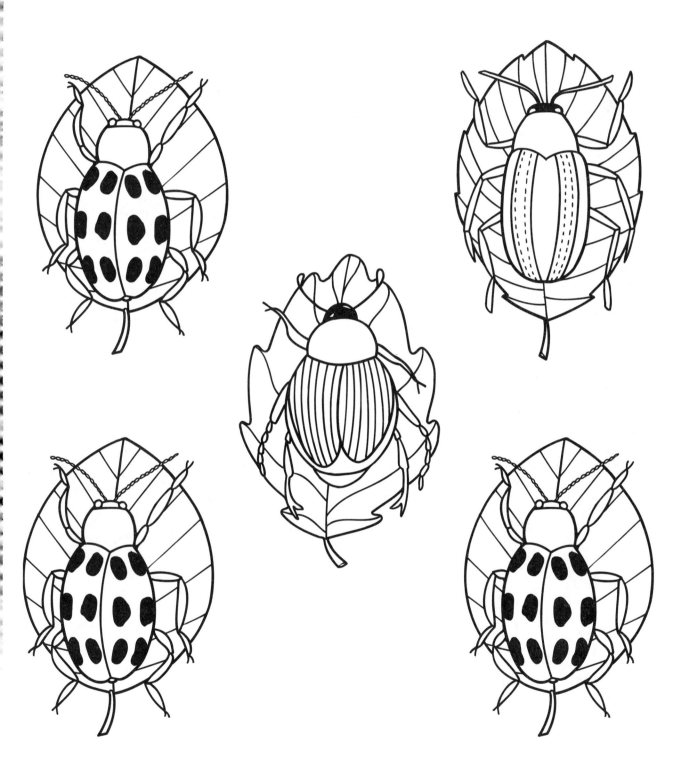

Name _____

# Where Is My Home?

Trace each path. Color the pictures.

*Essential Skills and Practice Grade K*

Name _____

# Animal Sightings

Cut out each animal card below on the dotted lines. Glue each card under the picture of where you find the animal.

| water | land | sky |
|---|---|---|

| camel  | owl  | dolphin  |
|---|---|---|
| lion  | parrot  | elephant  |
| whale  | zebra  | goose  |

*Essential Skills and Practice Grade K*

SCIENCE

Name _____

# A Long Time Ago

Color the scene. Then trace the letters below.

Dinosaurs lived a
long time ago.

*Essential Skills and Practice Grade K*

SCIENCE

Name _____

# Maiasaura Maze

Some dinosaurs made nests on the ground. They laid eggs in the nests. Baby dinosaurs hatched from the eggs.

Can you help Mother Maiasaura get back to her nest?
Draw a line to show her path. Watch out! T-Rex wants to eat her.

    *Essential Skills and Practice Grade K*

Name _____

# Long Gone

Connect the dots from **1** to **25**. Color.

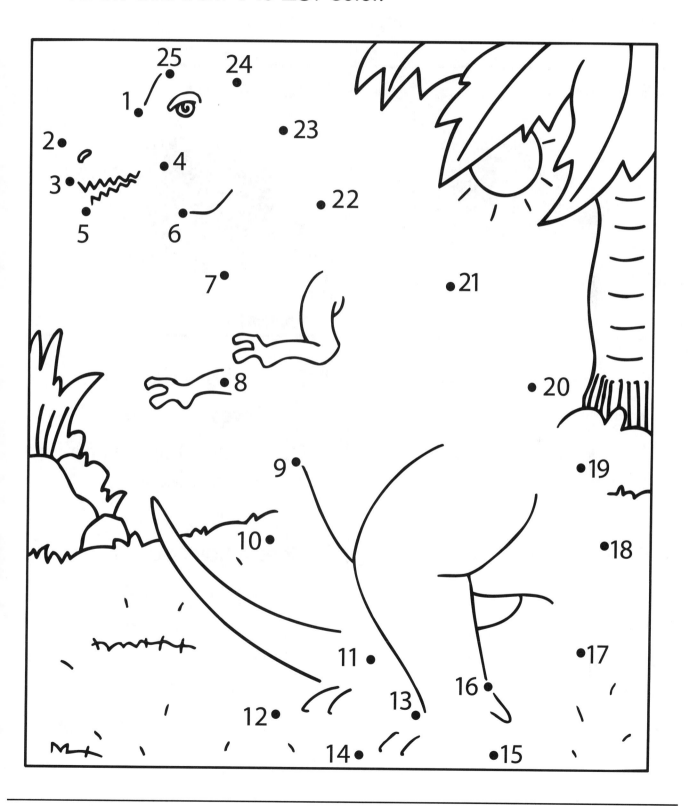

*Essential Skills and Practice Grade K*

Name _____

# Plant-Eater or Meat-Eater?

Some dinosaurs ate meat. Some dinosaurs ate plants. Look at the pictures. Circle yes or no to answer the questions.

**Allosaurus**

**Apatosaurus**

| | |
|---|---|
| 1. Does it have sharp teeth? | 1. Does it have sharp teeth? |
| yes　　　no | yes　　　no |
| 2. Does it stand upright on two strong back legs? | 2. Does it stand upright on two strong back legs? |
| yes　　　no | yes　　　no |
| 3. Does it have claws? | 3. Does it have claws? |
| yes　　　no | yes　　　no |
| If the answers are yes, circle meat-eater. If the answers are no, circle plant-eater. | If the answers are yes, circle meat-eater. If the answers are no, circle plant-eater. |
| meat-eater　　　plant-eater | meat-eater　　　plant-eater |

Name _____

# Seasons

Color the pictures. Trace and say the season words.

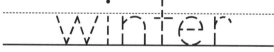

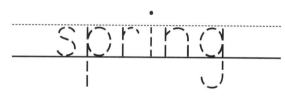

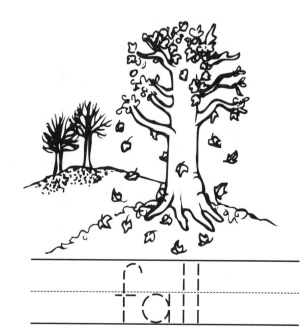

Name _____

# Spring, Summer, Fall, Winter

Number the events in order. Write a number in each box. Then color the pictures.

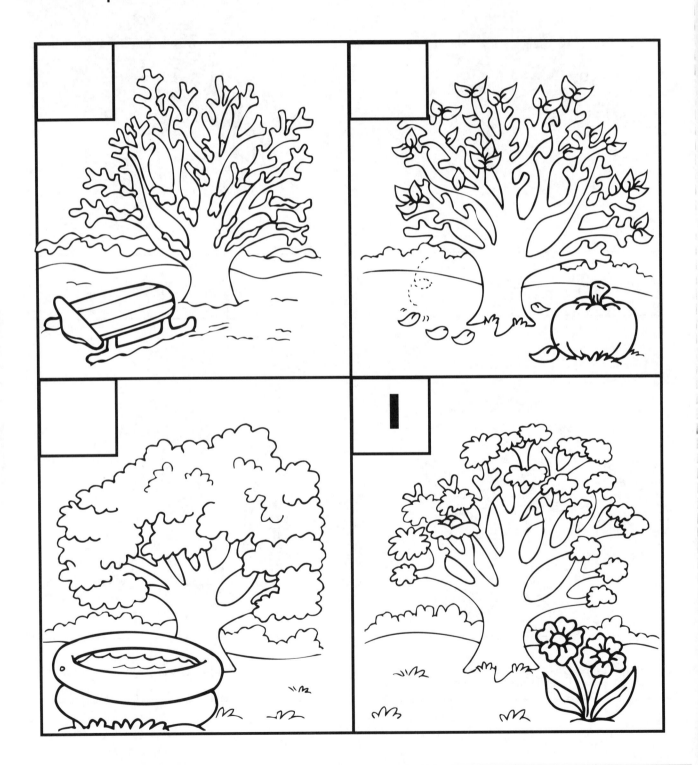

*Essential Skills and Practice Grade K*

Name _____

# Fall Scramble

Unscramble the fall word on each leaf. Color the leaf the correct color.

aotc

_ _ _ _

red

ndwi

_ _ _ _

blue

oancr

_ _ _ _ _

purple

eter

_ _ _ _

green

aleevs

_ _ _ _ _ _

brown

lbotaofl

_ _ _ _ _ _ _ _

orange

aerk

_ _ _ _

yellow

ohoslc

_ _ _ _ _ _

black

| | |
|---|---|
| acorn | coat |
| football | rake |
| school | tree |
| wind | leaves |

*Essential Skills and Practice Grade K*

Name _____

# Winter Word Search

Circle each winter word from the word box in the puzzle. Check off each word as you find it. Words go across and down.

- ☐ flakes
- ☐ skate
- ☐ January
- ☐ blizzard
- ☐ snow
- ☐ ice
- ☐ sled
- ☐ snowman
- ☐ mittens
- ☐ cold
- ☐ freeze
- ☐ ski

| r | f | r | a | m | k | l | i | n | x |
| s | l | e | d | n | f | k | c | k | v |
| J | a | n | u | a | r | y | e | i | c |
| s | k | a | t | e | e | b | g | s | o |
| n | e | g | f | t | e | t | s | g | l |
| o | s | b | l | i | z | z | a | r | d |
| w | m | i | t | t | e | n | s | s | r |
| b | i | m | s | k | i | y | o | k | o |
| s | n | o | w | m | a | n | g | y | v |

224

Name _____

# How Is the Weather?

Trace and color.

_____
sunny

_____
cloudy

_____
rainy

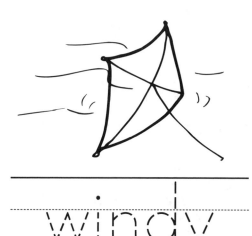

_____
windy

How is the weather today?

_____

_____

_____ .

225      *Essential Skills and Practice Grade K*

Name _____

# Weather Words

Circle the words. The words go → and ↓.

| f | r | d | l | w | i | n | d | y |
|---|---|---|---|---|---|---|---|---|
| z | a | r | i | a | o | c | w | b |
| r | i | u | t | b | t | l | g | s |
| s | n | o | w | y | s | o | y | u |
| u | y | s | a | n | q | u | j | n |
| x | k | p | r | n | w | d | e | n |
| h | c | v | m | i | n | y | m | y |

 warm

 snowy

 rainy

 cloudy

 sunny

 windy

226                    *Essential Skills and Practice Grade K*

Name _____

# Cold or Warm?

Look at the clothes each child is wearing.
Circle **cold** if the child is dressed for cold weather.
Circle **warm** if the child is dressed for warm weather.

cold        warm

cold        warm

cold        warm

cold        warm        cold        warm

SCIENCE

227                    *Essential Skills and Practice Grade K*

Name _____

# How Does It Feel Outside?

Write a word for each picture.

| hot | warm | cold |

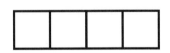

How does it feel outside today?

_____

---------------------------------

_____

Name _____

# Rain or Shine

Look at each weather forecast on the left and draw a line to show what the girl should wear.

*Essential Skills and Practice Grade K*

Name _____

# Off to Space!

Connect the dots from **1** to **25**. Color to finish the picture.

*Essential Skills and Practice Grade K*

Name _____

# Far Out!

Circle the words. The words go → and ↓.

| e | s | r | i | o | r | b | i | t |
|---|---|---|---|---|---|---|---|---|
| o | p | l | p | k | d | v | g | r |
| x | a | t | l | e | h | m | j | o |
| m | c | w | a | f | i | o | r | c |
| y | e | s | n | t | n | o | c | k |
| b | k | h | e | y | p | n | f | e |
| s | h | u | t | t | l | e | y | t |

 rocket

 moon

 space

 orbit

 planet

 shuttle

SCIENCE

*Essential Skills and Practice Grade K*

# My Name

Write your name.


First name

_____

- - - - - - - - - - - - - - - - - - - - - - - - - - -

_____


Middle name

_____

- - - - - - - - - - - - - - - - - - - - - - - - - - -

_____


Last name

_____

- - - - - - - - - - - - - - - - - - - - - - - - - - -

_____

Name _____

# Baby Days

Draw a picture of yourself when you were a baby.

Circle.

I was born on a _____.

**Monday**     **Tuesday**     **Wednesday**
**Thursday**     **Friday**     **Saturday**     **Sunday**

I am the _____ child in my family.

    **first**     **second**     **third**     **fourth**     **fifth**

SOCIAL STUDIES

Name _____

# Happy Birthday

Draw candles to show how old you are.

_____

I am _____ years old.

My birthday is

_____

_____.

*Essential Skills and Practice Grade K*

Name _____

# Look What I Can Do!

Put a ✓ in the box if you do the activity each day.

| | | |
|---|---|---|
| Eat | | |
| Get dressed | | |
| Brush teeth | | |
| Take a bath | | |
| Go to school | | |
| Play | | |
| Read books | | |
| Watch TV | | |
| Go to bed | | |

SOCIAL STUDIES

*Essential Skills and Practice Grade K*

Name _____

# Getting Bigger Each Day

Color the things that you can do now. Circle the things that you want to learn to do. Continue on the next page.

Name _____

*Essential Skills and Practice Grade K*

SOCIAL STUDIES

Name _____

# Things I Like to Do

Say the words.
Color the pictures of the things you like to do.

jump        sing        cook

write        skip        swim

Name _____

# My Favorite Toy

Draw a picture of your favorite toy.

Color other toys you like.

Name _____

# My Family Laughs!

Draw a picture showing something that makes your family laugh.

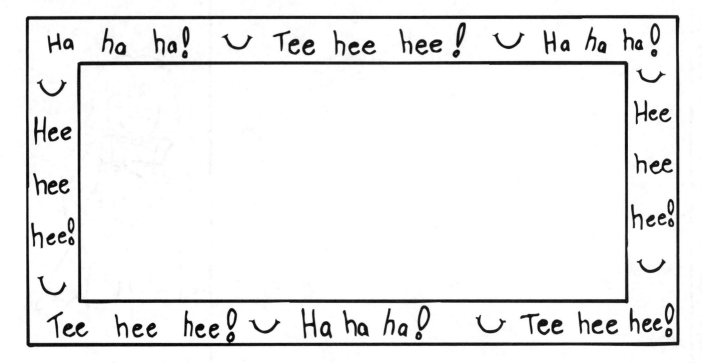

Color the things that make you laugh.

*Essential Skills and Practice Grade K*

Name _____

# I Can Get Mad

Color the pictures that make you feel mad.

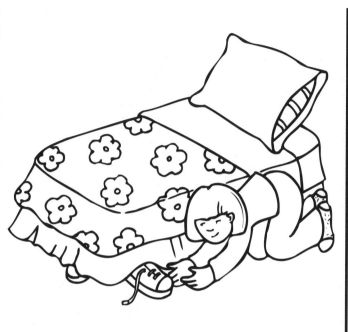

SOCIAL STUDIES

Name _____

# I Get Scared

Color the pictures of things that scare you.

# My Family

Trace the words. Draw a picture of your family.

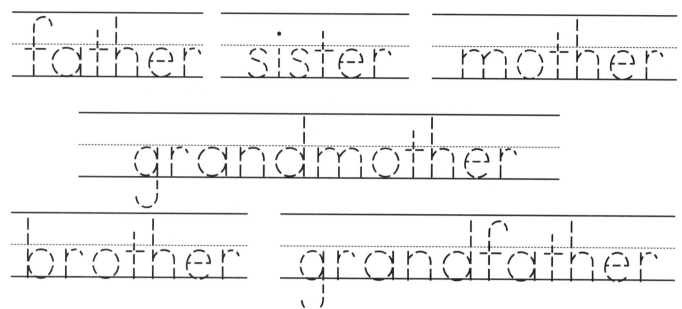

father    sister    mother

grandmother

brother    grandfather

*Essential Skills and Practice Grade K*

SOCIAL STUDIES

Name _____

# We Do Things Together

Look at each picture. If your family likes to do what is shown, color the picture.

Name _____

*Essential Skills and Practice Grade K*

SOCIAL STUDIES

Name _____

# My Jobs

Color the pictures of the jobs you do.

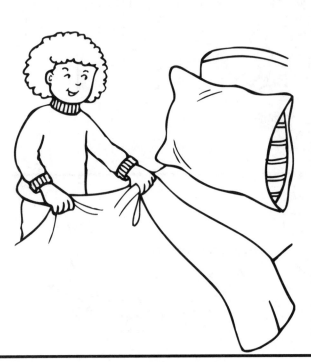

*Essential Skills and Practice Grade K*

Name _____

# When I Am Older

Color the pictures of the jobs that you would like to do someday.

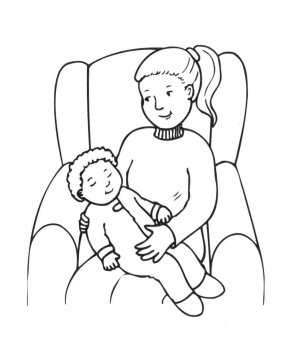

247      *Essential Skills and Practice Grade K*

Name _____

# I Play Inside

Color the things you could play with inside.
Draw an X on the things you could not play with inside.

Name _____

# Indoor and Outdoor Fun

Color the things you use inside yellow. Color the things you use outside blue.

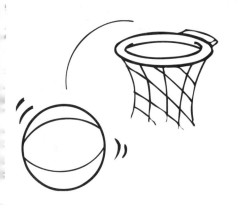 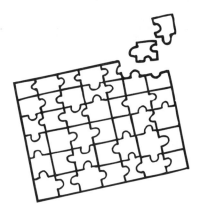 

  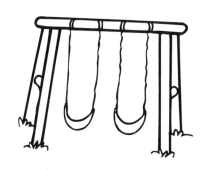

*Essential Skills and Practice Grade K*

Name _____

# My Friends

Draw a picture of two of your friends.

My friends' names are _____

_____

and _____

_____

We like to _____

# Friends Are Polite

Look at each picture.
Write the polite sentences next to the matching pictures.

Say this if you ask for something.

Say this if your friend gives you something.

Say this if you hurt your friend's feelings.

**Thank you!**   **I'm sorry.**   **Please.**

SOCIAL STUDIES

*Essential Skills and Practice Grade K*

Name _____

# Friends Have Fun

Draw a line to the picture that completes the sentence.

banana

You may ride my _____.

letter

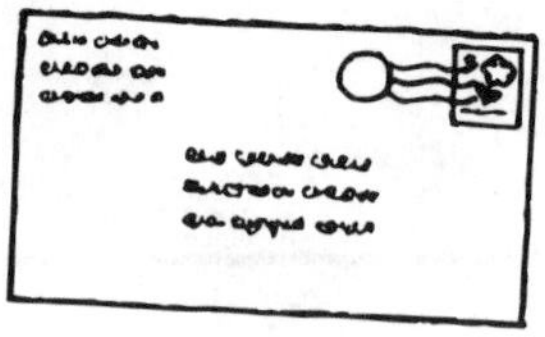

Have a bite of this _____.

bicycle

You may pet the _____.

ball

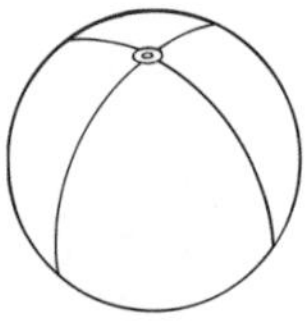

I will write you a _____.

cat

I will throw the _____.

Name _____

# Chef Charlie

Chef Charlie tossed the pizza crust. Where did it go?

*Essential Skills and Practice Grade K*

Name _____

# When I Grow Up

Color the pictures that show what you might be when you grow up.

Name _____

When I grow up, I want to be a
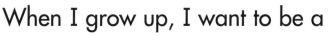

_____

_____

_____

*Essential Skills and Practice Grade K*

Name _____

# Learning the Past

Help the museum guide find the dinosaur display.

*Essential Skills and Practice Grade K*

Name _____

# To the Rescue

Connect the dots from **A** to **Z**. Color.

*Essential Skills and Practice Grade K*

Name _____

# Places

Draw lines to show where each item belongs.
Say the names of the places.

farm

bed

park bench

park

house

desk

tractor

school

What is your favorite place?

_____

_____

*Essential Skills and Practice Grade K*

Name _____

# A Busy Day

Circle the things that are in the picture.

Name _____

# Off to School

Connect the dots from **A** to **Z**.

*Essential Skills and Practice Grade K*

Name _____

# A Classroom

Finish each sentence with the name of what you see.

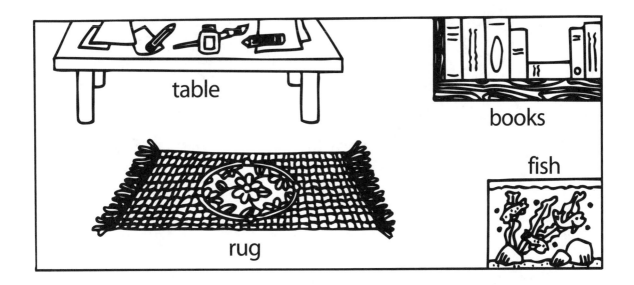

table

books

fish

rug

_____

You will go to the _____ .

_____

You will go to the _____ .

_____

You will go to the _____ .

_____

You will go to the _____ .

*Essential Skills and Practice Grade K*

SOCIAL STUDIES

Name _____

# School Time

Color the pictures. Check off the boxes of the things you do at school.

☐ sing

☐ draw

☐ count

☐ paint

☐ read

☐ write

Name _____

# Playground Fun

Trace the words.

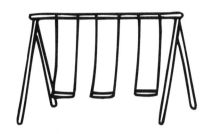

swing

climb

slide

kick

What do you like to do at the playground?

_____

_____

_____

*Essential Skills and Practice Grade K*

Name _____

# Safety Sign Match

Draw a line from each safety sign to its shadow.

railroad
crossing

no
bicycles

school
crossing

bicycle
crossing

stop

*Essential Skills and Practice Grade K*

Name _____

# Workers Use Transportation

Draw lines to match the pictures.

*Essential Skills and Practice Grade K*

SOCIAL STUDIES

Name _____

# Words to Know

Look at the picture. Read the words.
Write the words on the lines.

boat

bus

plane

car

bike

truck

*Essential Skills and Practice Grade K*

Name _____

# A Busy Street

Look at the picture. Write **3** things that people ride.

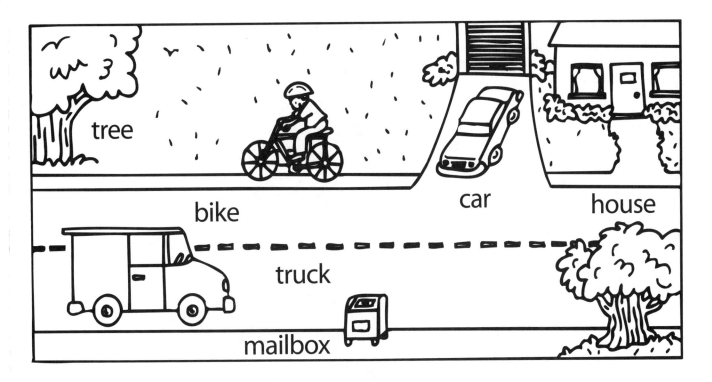

1. _____

2. _____

3. _____

*Essential Skills and Practice Grade K*

**SOCIAL STUDIES**

Name _____

# Let's Go!

Color the spaces with words for ways to travel.

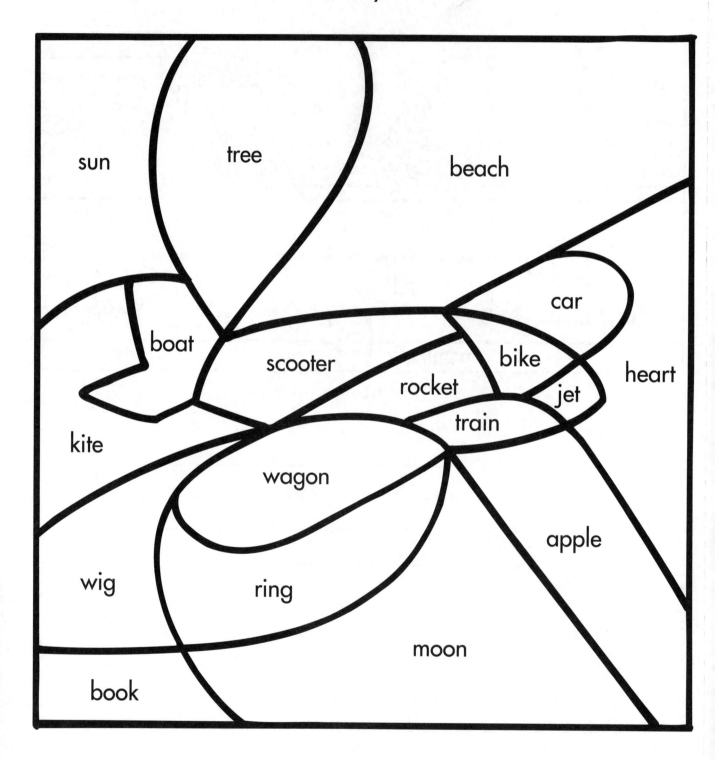

sun

tree

beach

car

boat

scooter

bike

rocket

jet

heart

kite

train

wagon

apple

wig

ring

moon

book

*Essential Skills and Practice Grade K*

Name _____

# Look and Find

Find three kinds of transportation.
Trace each one with a different color.

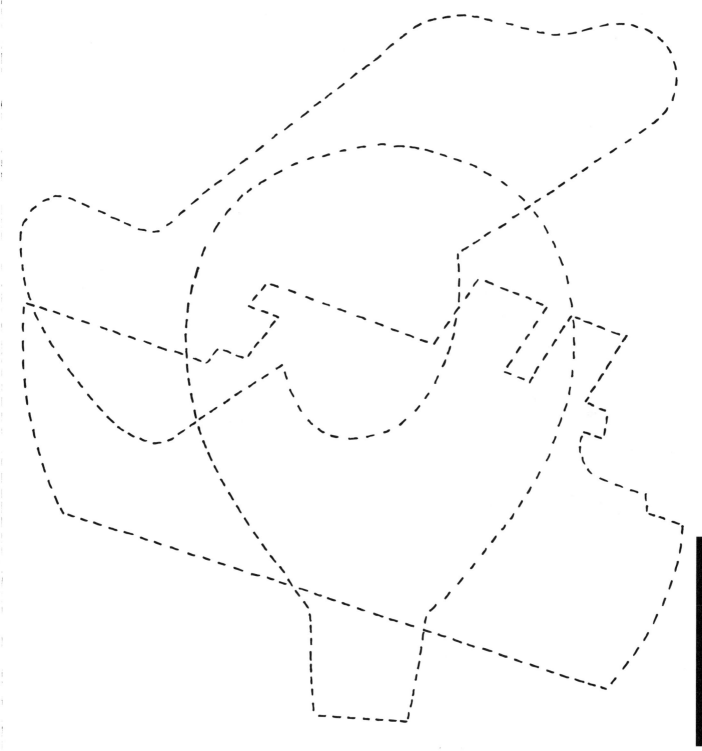

*Essential Skills and Practice Grade K*

Name _____

# On the Go!

Draw a line from each picture to the word that describes what it travels on. Then color the pictures.

| air | water | land |
|-----|-------|------|

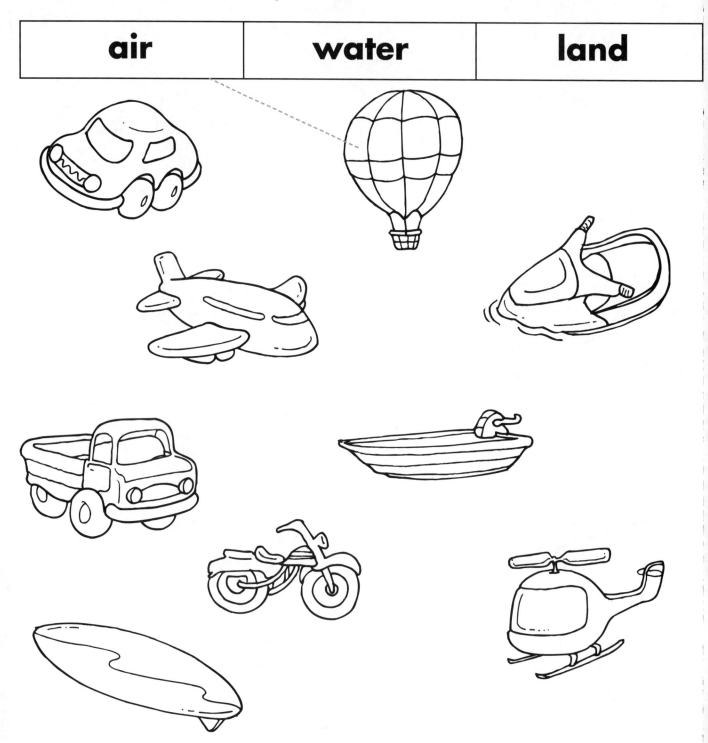

*Essential Skills and Practice Grade K*

Name _____

# Getting There

Check off each kind of transportation you have used. Draw a circle around a kind of transportation you would like to try some day.

☐ bicycle            ☐ train            ☐ horse & wagon

☐ ferry             ☐ airplane         ☐ boat

☐ car               ☐ subway           ☐ helicopter

☐ semitrailer       ☐ bus              ☐ camel

☐ streetcar         ☐ snowmobile       ☐ skateboard

*Essential Skills and Practice Grade K*

SOCIAL STUDIES

Name _____

# Going on a Trip

Where would you like to go on a trip? Draw it.
Trace and finish the sentence.

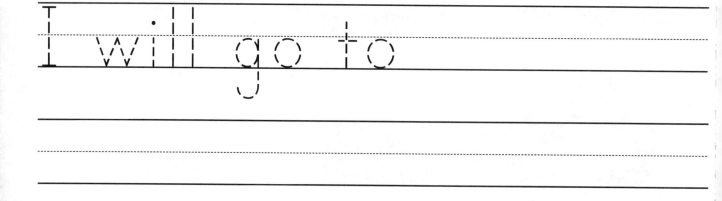

I will go to

*Essential Skills and Practice Grade K*

Name _____

# Color the things that you will take on your trip.

SOCIAL STUDIES

Name _____

# Away We Go

Circle and write the best title for each picture.

The Big Plane

Trains Are Fun

Going to Camp

_____

A Snowy Day

On Our Boat

At the Zoo

_____

_____

 Essential Skills and Practice Grade K

Name _____

# If I Could Go Anywhere

Draw a picture to show where you would like to visit.

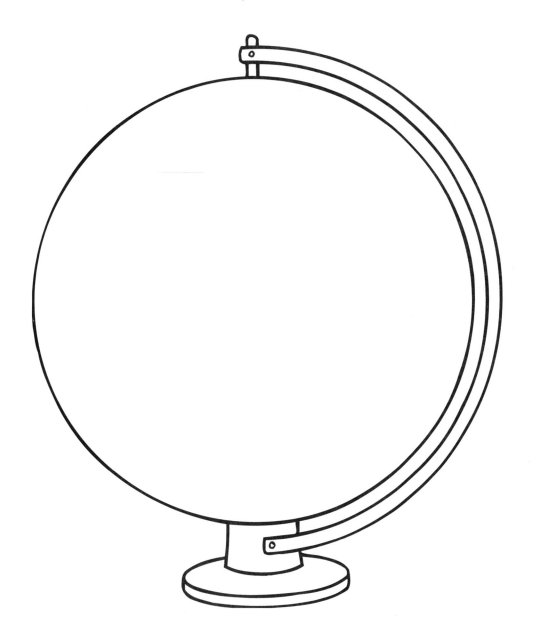

I would like to visit

_____

- - - - - - - - - - - - - - - - - - - - - - - - - - - - - - - -

_____

SOCIAL STUDIES

Name _____

# Halloween Puzzle

Read each clue. Write the correct word in the puzzle space.

**Down**

1. You wear me.

3. I taste good on apples.

4. I spin my own home.

**Across**

1. I am made of apples.

2. What you say on Halloween is "_____-or-treat"

5. I grow on a tree.

6. You get me on Halloween.

**Words**

cider

apple

costume

spider

trick

caramel

candy

*Essential Skills and Practice Grade K*

Name _____

# Leprechaun Puppet

On St. Patrick's Day, people wear green and put leprechauns in their windows. Color, cut, and glue pieces on a paper lunch bag. Use for puppet plays.

I Love Green!

SOCIAL STUDIES

Name _____

# Search for Spring Holiday Words

Circle each spring word in the word search.
Check off each word on the list as you find it in the puzzle.
Words go across and down.

| bunny |
| tree |
| chocolate |
| bonnet |
| carrot |
| hop |
| rain |
| egg |
| grass |
| grow |
| flower |
| rabbit |
| chick |
| basket |
| candy |
| sun |

| H | C | H | O | C | O | L | A | T | E |
|---|---|---|---|---|---|---|---|---|---|
| F | K | I | E | A | E | S | C | P | Z |
| L | S | U | N | R | E | T | K | R | B |
| O | V | E | C | R | A | B | B | I | T |
| W | M | T | H | O | P | C | U | R | R |
| E | G | G | I | T | O | A | N | A | E |
| R | R | X | C | F | M | N | N | I | E |
| B | A | S | K | E | T | D | Y | N | B |
| S | S | G | R | O | W | Y | T | C | J |
| T | S | D | B | O | N | N | E | T | S |

*Essential Skills and Practice Grade K*

SOCIAL STUDIES

Name _____

# A Special Day

Color the pictures that show things your family uses to celebrate a special holiday.

*Essential Skills and Practice Grade K*

Name _____

# My Holiday Dream

Write about a holiday dream.

_____

_____

_____

_____

_____

_____

_____

*Essential Skills and Practice Grade K*

Name _____

# Don't Litter

Color the picture of the seashore. Then put a big **X** on all the trash that should go in the trash can. There are five pieces of trash.

*Essential Skills and Practice Grade K*

Name _____

# City or Village Life

Color the pictures that show city life **blue**. Color the pictures that show village life **orange**. Color the pictures that can be village or city life **red**.

SOCIAL STUDIES

# Mountain Maze

One of Maria's chores is collecting reeds for weaving baskets. Help Maria find her way through the mountain trails to get to the river bank where the reeds grow.

# Answer Key

**Sailing Away**
Connect the dots from **A** to **Z**.

1

**Let's Play Leapfrog**
Help the girl find her way to the frog exhibit. Color the path in order from **N** to **Z**.

2

**Sailing Away**
Follow the alphabet to lead the pig to the radio.

3

**Fantastic Farm**
Find the letters from **a** to **m**. Color them.
a b c d e f g h i j k l m

4

**Trace and Write**
Trace the letters. Then write each letter.

Aa Aa Bb Bb
Cc Cc Dd Dd
Ee Ee Ff Ff
Gg Gg Hh Hh

A B C

5

**Trace and Write**
Trace the letters. Then write each letter.

Ii Ii Jj Jj
Kk Kk Ll Ll
Mm Mm Nn Nn
Oo Oo Pp Pp

I J K

6

**Trace and Write**
Trace the letters. Then write each letter.

Qq Qq Rr Rr
Ss Ss Tt Tt
Uu Uu Vv Vv
Ww Ww Xx Xx
Yy Yy Zz Zz

X Y Z

7

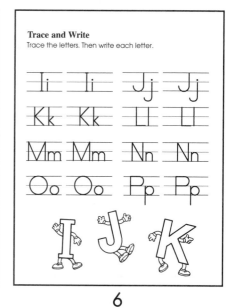

**Letter Trucks**
Write the letter that comes between.

W [X] Y

Q [R] S

K [L] M

B [C] D

D [E] F

F [G] H

8

**Letter Matchup**
In each row, circle the letters that match the first letter.

B B B R P
C Q O C C
D D P D O
F P F E F

9

285                                    *Essential Skills and Practice Grade K*

**More Matching**

In each row, circle the letters that match the first letter.

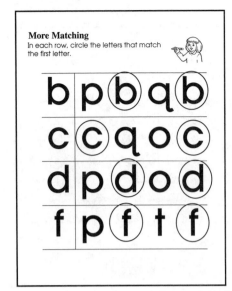

**Letter Garden**

Draw lines between the flowers to match the uppercase and lowercase letters.

Aa Bb Cc Dd Ee Ff Gg Hh Ii
Jj Kk Ll Mm Nn Oo Pp Qq Rr
Ss Tt Uu Vv Ww Xx Yy Zz

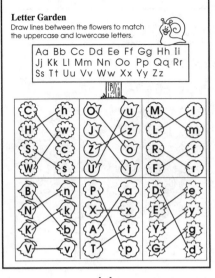

**I Can Match Letters**

Draw a line from each child to the matching lowercase letter.

10

11

12

**Follow the Path**

Say the alphabet. Write the missing letters.

**A Lost Ball**

Help Tommy find his ball.
Follow the words in ABC order.

**Hungry Birds**

Help the birds find the worms.
Color the boxes in ABC order.

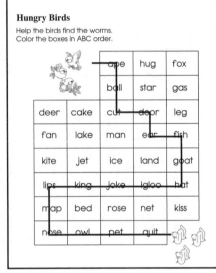

13

14

15

**New Word Fun**

Write the first letter for each picture.
Write the letters in the boxes to make a new word.

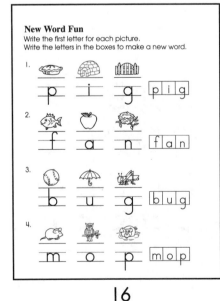

**Fill Them In**

Write the vowels to complete each word.

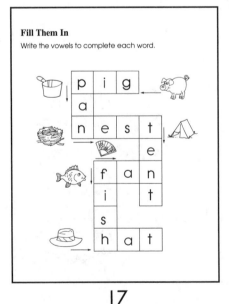

**The Sound of C**

Draw a line from each cat to a picture that begins with the sound of **c**.

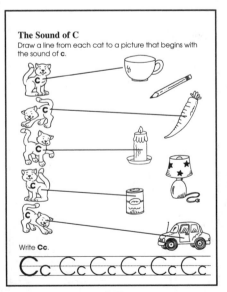

Write **Cc**.

16

17

18

*Essential Skills and Practice Grade K*

### The Sound of G

Color the pictures that begin with the sound of **g**.

Write **Gg**.

Gg Gg Gg Gg Gg

19

### The Sound of L

Look at the living room. Draw a circle around five things that begin with the sound of **L**. Color the picture.

Write **Ll**.

20

### Rain, Rain, Go Away

Find these things, which begin with **m**. Color them brown. Then color the rest of the picture.

mouse    monkey    mop    milk    mask

21

### Water Lover

Find these things, which begin with **r**. Color them orange. Then color the rest of the picture

rose    rake    ring    rocket    raccoon

22

### Plump Pig

Color each **u** purple. Then color the rest of the picture.

23

### The Sound of Y

Look at each picture. If it begins with **y**, circle **yes**. If it does not, circle **no**.

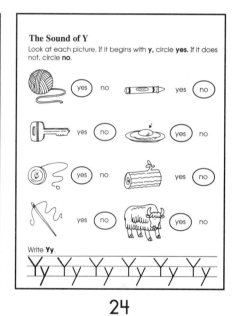

Write **Yy**.

Yy Yy Yy Yy Yy Yy

24

### All Kinds of Animals

Look at each animal. Say its name. Circle the sound you hear at the beginning of the word.

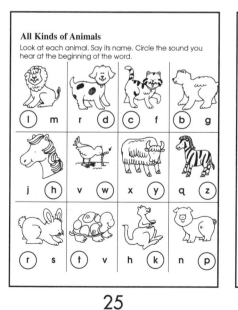

25

### Food Fun

Look at the first picture in each row. Say its name. Then color the picture that has the same beginning sound.

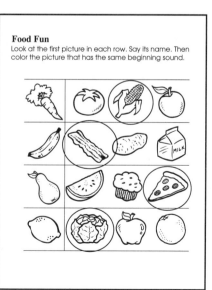

26

### Listen Carefully

Look at each column. Color the pictures that begin with the letter shown at the top.

27

*Essential Skills and Practice Grade K*

**Matching Sounds**
Draw lines from each letter to the pictures with the same beginning sound.

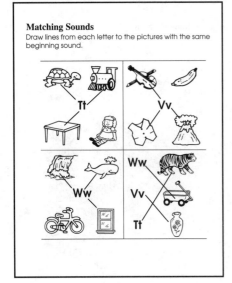

**Floating High**
Color the words that start with **e** orange.
Color the words that start with **f** yellow.
Write the words under the correct beginning letters below.

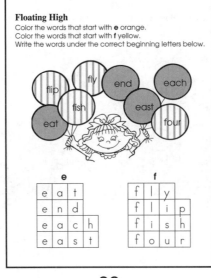

**Scrambled J's, K's, and L's**
Unscramble the words that name the pictures.
Write the words.

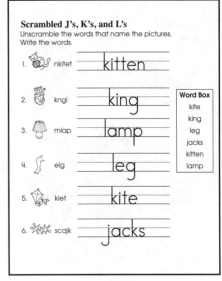

1. nkitet   kitten
2. kngi   king
3. mlap   lamp
4. elg   leg
5. kiet   kite
6. scajk   jacks

**Word Box**
kite
king
leg
jacks
kitten
lamp

28     29     30

**Ending Sounds**
Listen for the ending sound of each picture. Write it at the end of each word.

bag   bus
cup
hen   mud

**More Ending Sounds**
Listen for the ending sound of each picture. Write it at the end of each word.

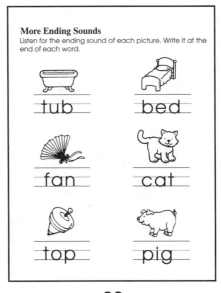

tub   bed
fan   cat
top   pig

**Beginning and End**
Say the names of the pictures. Write the letters that make the beginning and ending sounds.

cat   dog
fan   mop
bed   sun

31     32     33

**Discovering Differences**
Circle the animal that is different in each column.

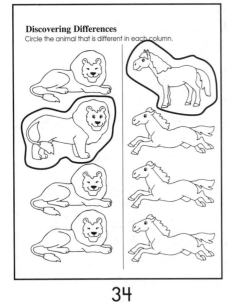

**Missing Parts**
Some of these elephants are missing body parts! Look at elephant **A** to see what s missing on the others. Name the missing body parts and draw them on the animals.

**Parts and Wholes**
Complete each picture by drawing the missing piece.

34     35     36

**What's Different?**
Can you find and circle ten ways the bottom picture is different?

37

**Opposite Matchup**
Draw lines to match the opposites.

38

**Ocean Opposites**
Draw lines to match the opposites.

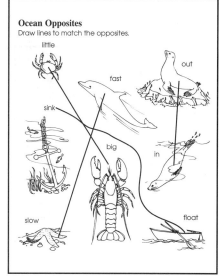

39

**Word Match**
Match each word with a picture.

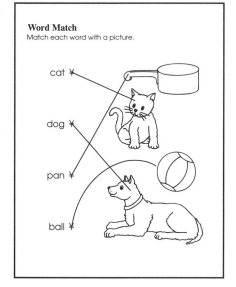

40

**Fun Word Match**
Match each word with a picture.

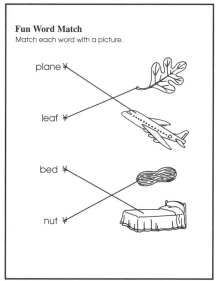

41

**Matching Words**
Circle matching pairs of words.

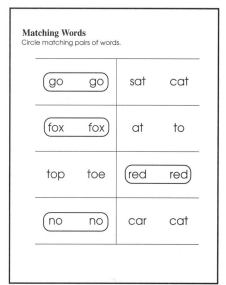

42

**I Read Words**
In each box, circle the words that match the word at the top.

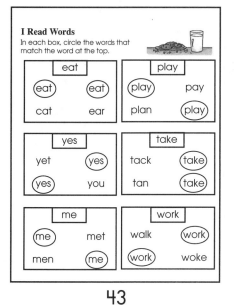

43

**Final Question**
Match the scrambled letters to find out what the farmer wants to ask.

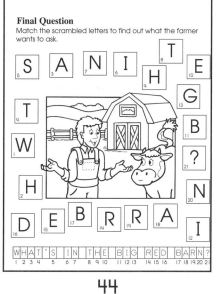

44

**A Plane**
Write the sentence.

See the plane go up.

45

*Essential Skills and Practice Grade K*

## Word Match
Circle the words that match the words at the top of each box.

| red sled | fun ride |
| --- | --- |
| red slide | fun ride |
| **(red sled)** | fan ride |

| wet kid | hot fire |
| --- | --- |
| well kid | **(hot fire)** |
| **(wet kid)** | hot find |

46

## A Secret Sentence
Color the following words in the puzzle **green**.

camp   when   test   time

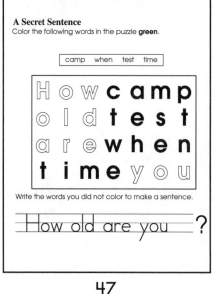

Write the words you did not color to make a sentence.

How old are you ?

47

## Look and Color
Color the following words red.

the   was   on   and   but

Write the words you did not color to make a sentence.

What is your name ?

48

## New Words
Color the picture. Add the letter. Write the word.

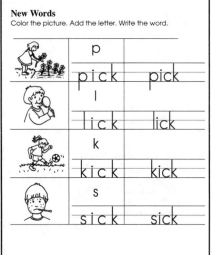

| p | | |
| --- | --- | --- |
| pick | pick | |
| l | | |
| lick | lick | |
| k | | |
| kick | kick | |
| s | | |
| sick | sick | |

49

## Crack the Code
Write the missing letters for each word.
Use the code at the bottom of the page.

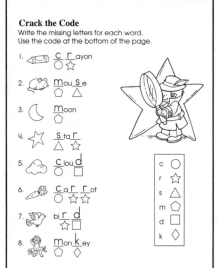

1. c_r_ayon
2. m_ou_s_e
3. m_oon
4. s_ta_r
5. c_lou_d
6. c_a_r_r_ot
7. bi_r_d
8. m_on_k_ey

| c | ○ |
| --- | --- |
| r | ☆ |
| s | △ |
| m | ⬠ |
| d | □ |
| k | ◇ |

50

## Double Trouble
Write each word in the box next to a word in the puzzle to make a new word.

| bell | walk | ground | room |
| --- | --- | --- | --- |
| box | ball | fish | print |

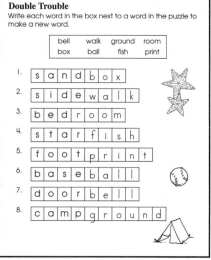

1. s a n d b o x
2. s i d e w a l k
3. b e d r o o m
4. s t a r f i s h
5. f o o t p r i n t
6. b a s e b a l l
7. d o o r b e l l
8. c a m p g r o u n d

51

## Figure Them Out
Unscramble each word. Be sure that it matches the meaning.

| teacher | ice cream | apple |
| --- | --- | --- |
| mouse | jogger | tennis |

1. Someone who runs is called a
   rjggeo  j o g g e r .
2. A game that uses a racket and a small ball is
   stinne  t e n n i s .
3. Something cold to eat on a hot day is
   cie ramec  i c e   c r e a m .
4. Someone who teaches children is a
   ehteac  t e a c h e r .
5. A tasty fruit that grows on a tree is called an
   leppa  a p p l e .
6. A furry little animal that squeaks is a
   somue  m o u s e .

52

## At the Bus Stop
Read each question. Answer the question aloud.
Trace the question mark at the end of the question.

Why are the people waiting?

Who has groceries?

Who has a newspaper?

How many kids are waiting?

53

## Is It a Question?
Read the sentence. Then repeat it. After repeating the sentence, tell whether it is a question or a statement.

1. My wagon is red. statement
2. The sky looks cloudy. statement
3. My favorite colors are red and blue. statement
4. Do you know where the store is? question
5. Is this a difficult activity? question
6. I am very tired today. statement
7. First I wake up and then I brush my teeth. statement
8. After school I like to play with my friends. statement
9. What time do you go to school? question
10. He helped her ride the bike last Saturday. statement

54

*Essential Skills and Practice Grade K*

### Words

Write the correct word on each line.

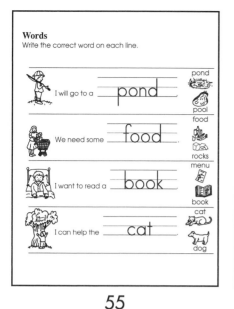

I will go to a ___pond___. — pond, pool

We need some ___food___. — food, rocks

I want to read a ___book___. — menu, book

I can help the ___cat___. — cat, dog

**55**

### Color Craze

Follow the directions for each coloring activity.

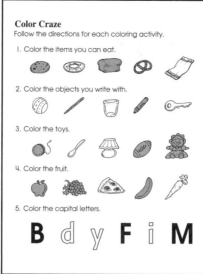

1. Color the items you can eat.

2. Color the objects you write with.

3. Color the toys.

4. Color the fruit.

5. Color the capital letters.

B d y F i M

**56**

### I Can Have Fun

Color the things that go together in each row.

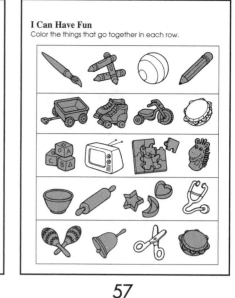

**57**

### In the Middle

Color each object that is in the middle.

**58**

### Top, Middle, Bottom

Look at the picture. Who is at the **top** of the hill? Who is at the **middle** of the hill? Who is at the **bottom** of the hill? Fill in the blanks below.

The dog is at the ___top___ of the hill.

The cat is at the ___middle___ of the hill.

The boy is at the ___bottom___ of the hill.

**59**

### In or Out

Look at each picture. Circle whether the clown is **in** or **out**.

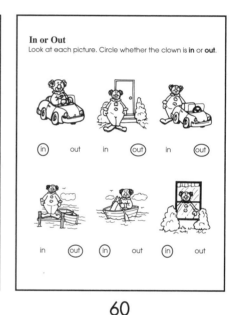

**60**

### More Color Words

Trace the words. Say the color names. Color the crayons.

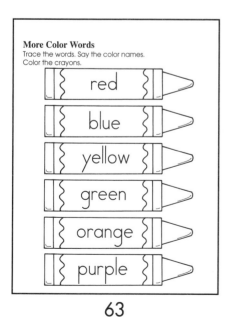

red

blue

yellow

green

orange

purple

**63**

### A Tisket, a Tasket

Follow the directions to color the basket.
1. Color one flower red.
2. Color one flower blue.
3. Draw a bow on the basket.
4. Color the basket green and yellow.
5. Draw another flower in the basket.

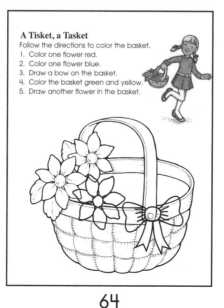

**64**

### Make a Picture

Follow the directions to complete the picture.

1. Draw a tree to the right of the school.

2. Draw a sun in the top left of the picture.

3. Draw a flag to the left of the school.

4. Draw some flowers to the right of the tree.

5. Draw a picture of yourself to the left of the school.

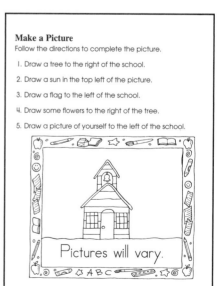

Pictures will vary.

**65**

*Essential Skills and Practice Grade K*

**I Enjoy Books**
Circle and write the best title for the picture.

Eating Dinner

Books for Sale

(We Like to Read)

We Like to Read

66

**Can It Really Happen?**
Does each picture show something that can really happen?
Circle **yes** if it does.
Circle **no** if it does not.

67

**Funny Garden**
Does each picture show something that can really happen?
Circle **yes** if it does.
Circle **no** if it does not.

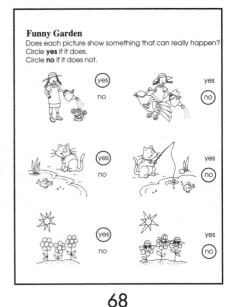

68

**Rhyme Time**
Color. Draw lines to match the rhyming words.

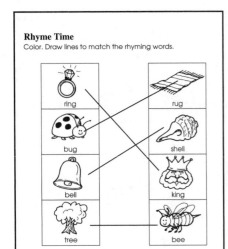

ring

rug

bug

shell

bell

king

tree

bee

69

**Time to Rhyme**
Use the picture clues to match the rhyming words.

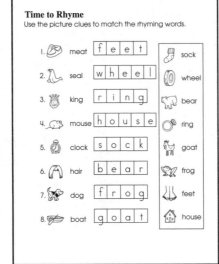

1. meat — f e e t — sock
2. seal — w h e e l — wheel
3. king — r i n g — bear
4. mouse — h o u s e — ring
5. clock — s o c k — goat
6. hair — b e a r — frog
7. dog — f r o g — feet
8. boat — g o a t — house

70

**Before and After**
Look at the picture in the middle. Draw something that happens before and after. Trace the words.

before

*Answers will vary.*

after

71

**Draw a Dinosaur**
These pictures are out of order. Number the steps from 1 to 6.

2 | 4

5 | 1

3 | 6

Follow the steps to draw a dinosaur.

72

**My Day at Kindergarten**
Read the story below. Then cut out and place the sentences in sequential order.

When the bell rings it is time to go inside. First, the teacher reads a story. Then we have a snack. Finally, we do an art project. At 12:00, it is time to go home.

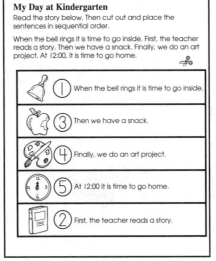

① When the bell rings it is time to go inside.

③ Then we have a snack.

④ Finally, we do an art project.

⑤ At 12:00 it is time to go home.

② First, the teacher reads a story.

73

**Sailing Fun**
Listen to a story about Matt and his dad.

Matt and his dad enjoy sailing. When they sail, they like to listen to music. Matt likes fast, loud music. His dad likes slow, soft music. Matt and his dad have lunch on the boat, too. Matt likes hot dogs. His dad likes ham sandwiches.

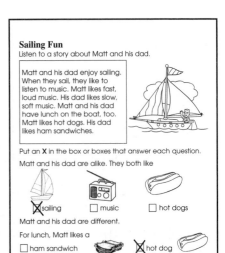

Put an **X** in the box or boxes that answer each question.

Matt and his dad are alike. They both like

[X] sailing   [ ] music   [ ] hot dogs

Matt and his dad are different.

For lunch, Matt likes a
[ ] ham sandwich   [X] hot dog

For lunch, his dad likes a
[X] ham sandwich   [ ] hot dog

75

*Essential Skills and Practice Grade K*

### What Happens Next
Draw a line to match the cause to the effect.

Cause       Effect

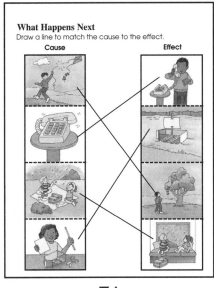

76

### I Can Circle What Happens Next
Circle the picture that shows what will happen next.

Daniel threw a stick across the yard for his dog, Muffy.    Muffy will take a nap.    Muffy will run to get the stick.

Rachel wrote a letter. She put it in an envelope and put a stamp on it.    Rachel will put the letter in the mailbox.    Rachel will put the letter in the bathtub.

The cake was cool. Tyler got the bowl of frosting.    Tyler will cut the cake.    Tyler will frost the cake.

77

### Size Search
Cut out the animal cards below. Glue each animal under the correct size.

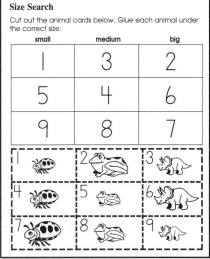

79

### The Pick of the Garden
Circle the animal that is biggest in each row.

Robin    Grasshopper    Beetle

Butterfly    Rabbit    Snail

Caterpillar    Hummingbird    Squirrel

80

### Perfectly Pleasing Patterns
Circle the object that comes next.
Color the pictures.

81

### Grow a Garden
Circle the item that comes next in each row.

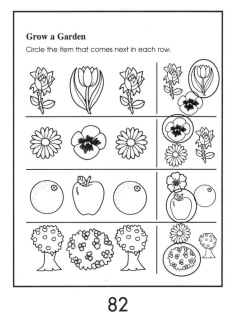

82

### Animal Parade
Circle the animal that comes next in each parade.

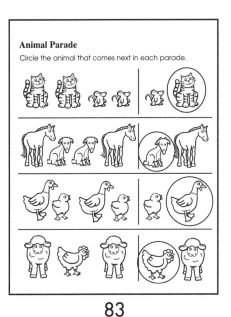

83

### Drawing Shapes

Trace.   Draw.     Trace.   Draw.

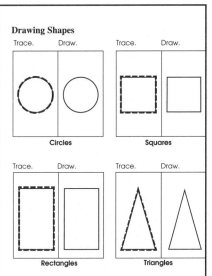

Circles      Squares

Trace.   Draw.     Trace.   Draw.

Rectangles      Triangles

84

### Floating Up
Color **6** ◯ orange.
Color **7** ☆ blue.

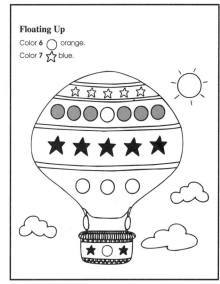

85

*Essential Skills and Practice Grade K*

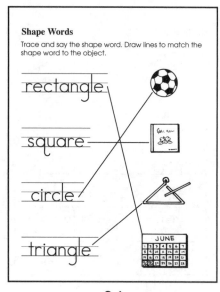

**Shape Words**

Trace and say the shape word. Draw lines to match the shape word to the object.

rectangle

square

circle

triangle

86

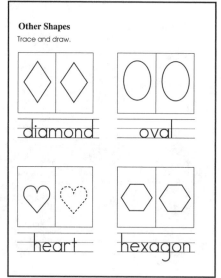

**Other Shapes**

Trace and draw.

diamond

oval

heart

hexagon

87

**Fun on the Farm**

Find the circles, triangles, and squares. Color them. Color the rest of the picture.

88

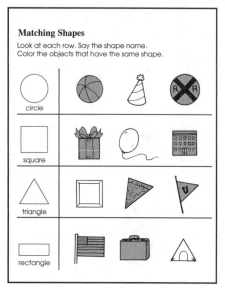

**Matching Shapes**

Look at each row. Say the shape name. Color the objects that have the same shape.

circle

square

triangle

rectangle

89

**A Yummy Number**

To find the mystery number, color the spaces with these numbers purple.

9   5   8   7   10   13   18   17   20   19   11

Circle the mystery number.   (5)   10   18

91

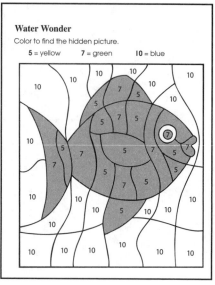

**Water Wonder**

Color to find the hidden picture.

**5** = yellow     **7** = green     **10** = blue

92

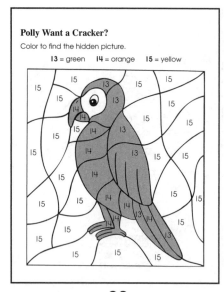

**Polly Want a Cracker?**

Color to find the hidden picture.

**13** = green   **14** = orange   **15** = yellow

93

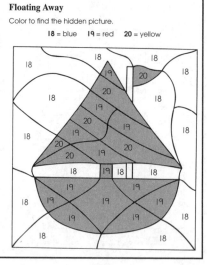

**Floating Away**

Color to find the hidden picture.

**18** = blue   **19** = red   **20** = yellow

94

**Count and Write**

Trace the numbers.

1  2  3  4  5
6  7  8  9  10

Write the numbers from 1 to 10.

1  2  3  4  5
6  7  8  9  10

1  2  3  4  5
6  7  8  9  10

95

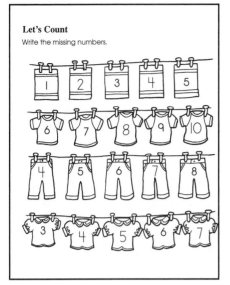

**Let's Count**
Write the missing numbers.

96

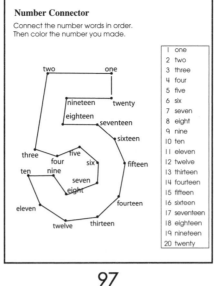

**Number Connector**
Connect the number words in order.
Then color the number you made.

| | |
|---|---|
| 1 | one |
| 2 | two |
| 3 | three |
| 4 | four |
| 5 | five |
| 6 | six |
| 7 | seven |
| 8 | eight |
| 9 | nine |
| 10 | ten |
| 11 | eleven |
| 12 | twelve |
| 13 | thirteen |
| 14 | fourteen |
| 15 | fifteen |
| 16 | sixteen |
| 17 | seventeen |
| 18 | eighteen |
| 19 | nineteen |
| 20 | twenty |

97

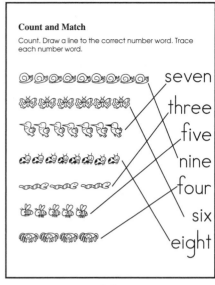

**Count and Match**
Count. Draw a line to the correct number word. Trace
each number word.

98

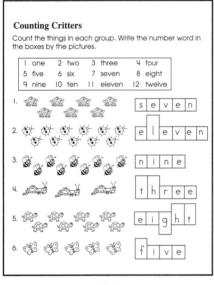

**Counting Critters**
Count the things in each group. Write the number word in
the boxes by the pictures.

99

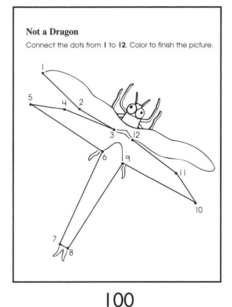

**Not a Dragon**
Connect the dots from 1 to 12. Color to finish the picture.

100

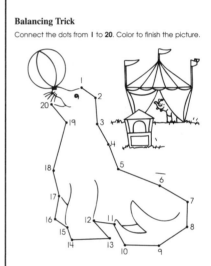

**Balancing Trick**
Connect the dots from 1 to 20. Color to finish the picture.

101

**In the Town Square**
Connect the dots to see what is in the town square.

102

**Making Music**
Color the sets of 3.

103

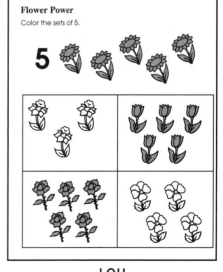

**Flower Power**
Color the sets of 5.

104

*Essential Skills and Practice Grade K*

**Mouse Lunch**

Find the food and color it green. Then color the rest of the picture.

Circle to show how many.

105

**Farm Count**

Count the objects. Write the number.

106

**Gardening Counting**

Count the objects. Write the number.
Circle the smaller number.

107

**Barnyard Hoedown**

Count the animals and trace the letters below. Color.

seven    eight

nine    ten

108

**Bird Buddies**

Find the numbers 1 to 10 in the picture. Color them.

109

**I Can Count**

Count and color.

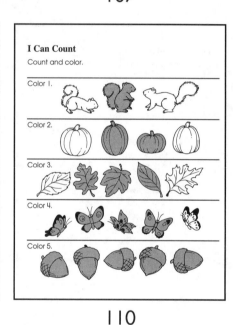

Color 1.

Color 2.

Color 3.

Color 4.

Color 5.

110

**It's a Ten**

Draw more objects to make ten in each set. Then color the pictures.

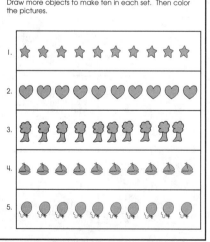

111

**Tally It Up**

Use tally marks to show how many objects are in each box.

| I | II | III | IIII | ‖‖ | ‖‖ I |
|---|----|-----|------|-----|------|
| 1 | 2  | 3   | 4    | 5   | 6    |

112

**Count the Objects**

Count. Circle the number.

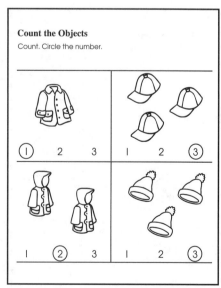

113

### Animals in Winter

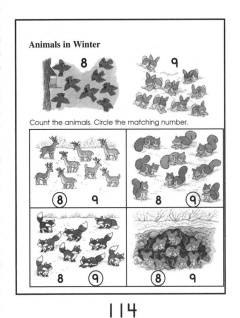

Count the animals. Circle the matching number.

### Super Circles

Count the circles. Color them.

Circle to show how many circles you found.

11  12  13  14  15  16  (17)  18  19  20

### Spotty Leopards

Circle the number of spots on each leopard.

114

115

116

### I Can Write Numbers

Trace. Count and circle the pictures.

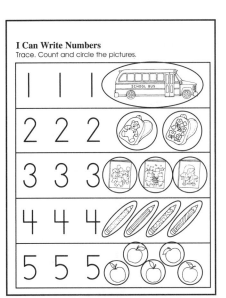

### Clean and Healthy

Trace the number that tells how many.

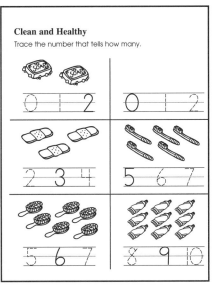

### Elephant Snacks

Count the peanuts in each bag.
Then write the number on the line.

117

118

119

### Stringing Numbers

On each string, draw enough beads to show
the number.

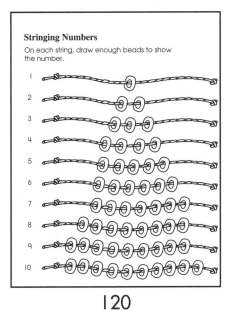

### Mouse Hunt

Find **10** mice below. Color them.
Color the rest of the picture.

120

121

*Essential Skills and Practice Grade K*

**Nut Hunt**

Find the nuts . Color them brown. Then color the rest of the picture. Can you find **11** nuts in all?

122

**Big Jumpers!**

Find the grasshoppers . Color them green. Then color the rest of the picture. Can you find **12** grasshoppers in all?

123

**Monkeying Around**

Find the bananas . Color them yellow. Then color the rest of the picture. Can you find **15** bananas in all?

124

**Color Creations**

Find the crayons . Color them purple. Then color the rest of the picture. Can you find **18** crayons in all?

125

**Feeding the Birds**

Draw **15** more pieces of birdseed in the bag. Then answer the question below.

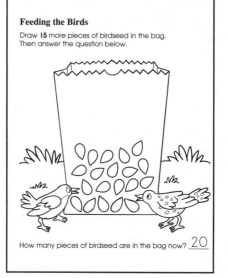

How many pieces of birdseed are in the bag now? __20__

126

**Clever Clover**

Look carefully at the picture. Find the **25** hidden shamrocks. Color them green.

127

**Fish Bowl**

Color **20** fish.

Circle to show how many fish are left over. ⑤ 6 7

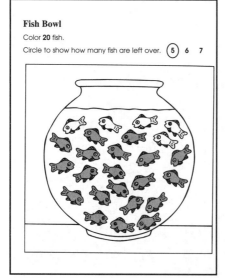

128

**Snail Garden**

Color **25** snails brown .

Circle to show how many snails are left over. ③ 4 5

129

*Essential Skills and Practice Grade K*

**Piggy Bank**

Color **24** pennies brown 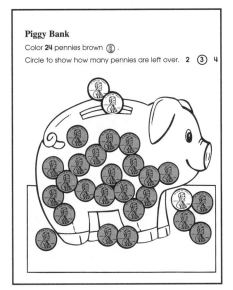.
Circle to show how many pennies are left over.  2  ③  4

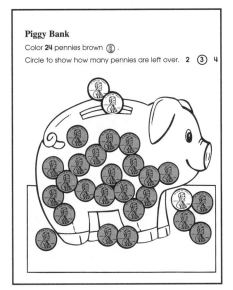

130

---

**Which Is More?**

Count the objects in each group. For each row, circle the group with the larger number. Then color the objects.

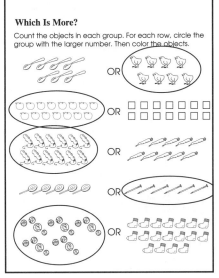

131

---

**Finding Friends**

Help Tommy Turtle find his friends. Color the path that goes in order from **1** to **8**.

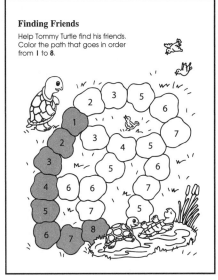

132

---

**I Can Play**

Draw a path to each toy by counting from 1 to 9.

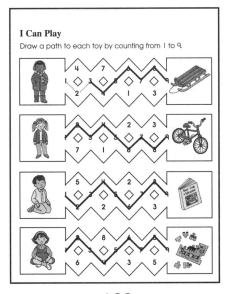

133

---

**Ready to Land**

Count from **1** to **20** to take the plane to the hangar.

134

---

**A–mazing Football**

Get Freddy Football to the end zone by counting by 2s. Starting with 2, color the footballs that contain numbers counting by 2 until you reach the end zone and score a touchdown.

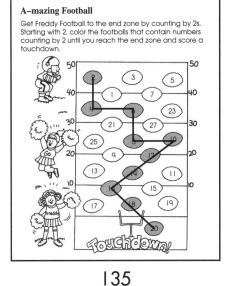

135

---

**Crazy Counting**

Trace. Write the missing numbers.

Count by twos.

2  4  6  8  10

Count by fives.

5  10  15  20  25

Count by tens.

10  20  30  40  50

136

---

**Add them Up**

Write the numbers that tell how many.

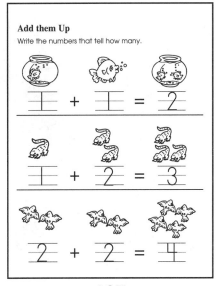

1 + 1 = 2

1 + 2 = 3

2 + 2 = 4

137

---

*Essential Skills and Practice Grade K*

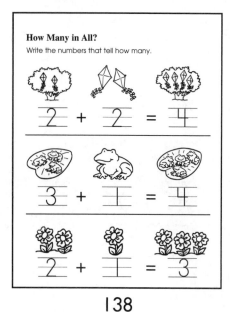

**How Many in All?**

Write the numbers that tell how many.

2 + 2 = 4

3 + 1 = 4

2 + 1 = 3

138

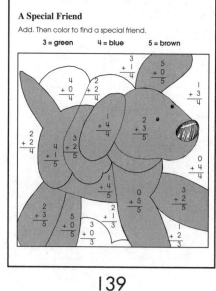

**A Special Friend**

Add. Then color to find a special friend.

3 = green     4 = blue     5 = brown

139

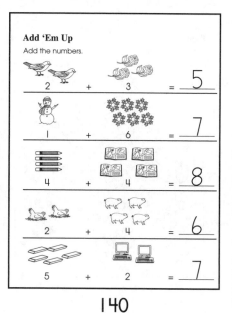

**Add 'Em Up**

Add the numbers.

2 + 3 = 5

1 + 6 = 7

4 + 4 = 8

2 + 4 = 6

5 + 2 = 7

140

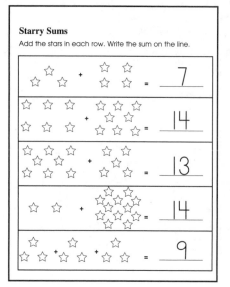

**Starry Sums**

Add the stars in each row. Write the sum on the line.

= 7

= 14

= 13

= 14

= 9

141

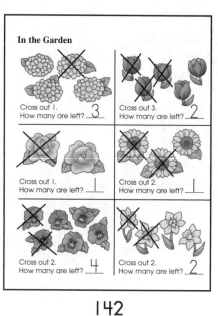

**In the Garden**

Cross out 1.
How many are left? 3

Cross out 3.
How many are left? 2

Cross out 1.
How many are left? 1

Cross out 2.
How many are left? 1

Cross out 2.
How many are left? 4

Cross out 2.
How many are left? 2

142

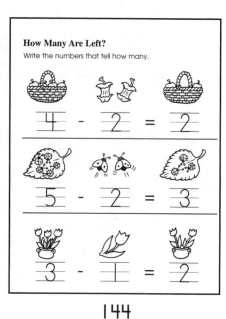

**How Many Are Left?**

Write the numbers that tell how many.

4 - 2 = 2

5 - 2 = 3

3 - 1 = 2

144

**Wholes and Halves**

Look at the vegetables at the bottom of the page. Draw two halves next to the matching whole vegetable.

whole     halves

whole     halves

whole     halves

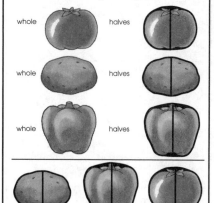

145

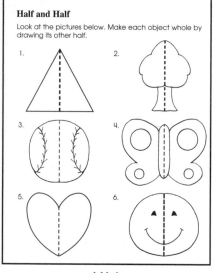

**Half and Half**

Look at the pictures below. Make each object whole by drawing its other half.

1.

2.

3.

4.

5.

6.

146

**Where's the Turtle?**

Write the place of the turtle.

first second third fourth fifth

first second third fourth fifth

first second third fourth fifth

first second third fourth fifth

**147**

**Friends Go Hiking**

The friends are following their leader on the trail.
Draw a line from each number-order word to the matching hiker.

fourth   third   first   second   eighth   fifth   seventh   sixth

**148**

**Money Mania**

Add the coin values in each row. Write the total amount on the line.

| penny 1¢ | nickel 5¢ | dime 10¢ | quarter 25¢ | |
|---|---|---|---|---|
| 1. | | | | = 2¢ |
| 2. | | | | = 7¢ |
| 3. | | | | = 30¢ |
| 4. | | | | = 16¢ |
| 5. | | | | = 30¢ |
| 6. | | | | = 30¢ |
| 7. | | | | = 30¢ |
| 8. | | | | = 12¢ |
| 9. | | | | = 19¢ |
| 10. | | | | = 36¢ |

**149**

**Money Matters**

Add the coin values in each row. Write the total amount on the line.

| penny 1¢ | nickel 5¢ | dime 10¢ | quarter 25¢ | |
|---|---|---|---|---|
| 1. | | | | = 11¢ |
| 2. | | | | = 20¢ |
| 3. | | | | = 45¢ |
| 4. | | | | = 31¢ |
| 5. | | | | = 17¢ |
| 6. | | | | = 50¢ |
| 7. | | | | = 9¢ |
| 8. | | | | = 25¢ |
| 9. | | | | = 27¢ |
| 10. | | | | = 45¢ |

**150**

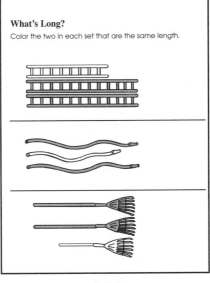

**What's Long?**

Color the two in each set that are the same length.

**151**

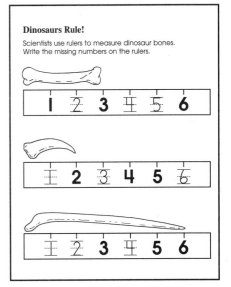

**Dinosaurs Rule!**

Scientists use rulers to measure dinosaur bones.
Write the missing numbers on the rulers.

1  2  3  4  5  6

1  2  3  4  5  6

1  2  3  4  5  6

**152**

**I Can Measure**

Draw a line from each child to the correct measuring tool.

What does Dan need to measure the sugar?

What does Jen need to weigh the oranges?

What does Jill need to measure how long the ribbon is?

What does Matt need to find out how cold it is?

**153**

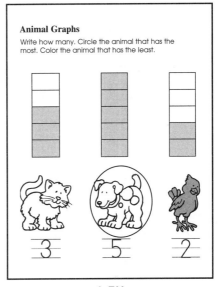

**Animal Graphs**

Write how many. Circle the animal that has the most. Color the animal that has the least.

3   5   2

**154**

*Essential Skills and Practice Grade K*

## Funny Frogs

Count the frogs and write the number.
Color a square for each frog.

2    3    4    3

## Days of the Week

Trace the words. Say them.

The first day of the week.

Sunday

The second day of the week.

Monday

The third day of the week.

Tuesday

The fourth day of the week.

Wednesday

## More Days of the Week

Trace the words. Say them.

The fifth day of the week.

Thursday

The sixth day of the week.

Friday

The seventh day of the week.

Saturday

What's your favorite day of the week?

Answers will vary.

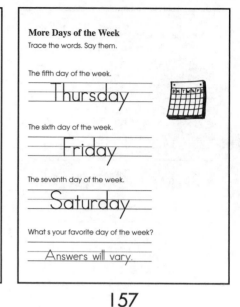

155    156    157

## Time of Day

Trace and color. Draw a picture of something you
do during each time of the day.

morning     Pictures will vary.

afternoon     Pictures will vary.

night     Pictures will vary.

## Body Parts

Point to the body parts. Say the name of each.
Trace the words.

head

arm

hand

leg

foot

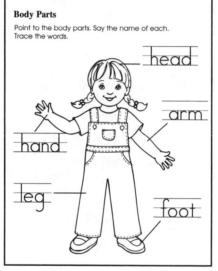

## Left and Right

Draw a ring on the right hand.
Draw a watch on the left wrist.

left        right

When you draw or write, which hand do you use?

Answers will vary.

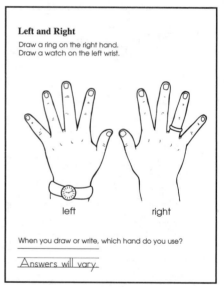

158    159    160

## My Hair

Draw a picture of your face and hair.

Answers will vary.

Circle.

My hair is _____.
straight   curly   wavy

The color is _____.
brown   black   red   blond

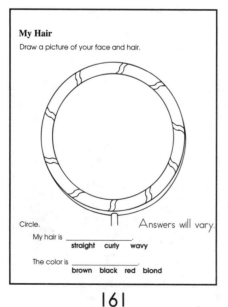

## My Feet

Draw a picture of your feet.

Pictures will vary.

Color the things that your feet help you do.

161    162

302                                    Essential Skills and Practice Grade K

## My Five Senses

Which parts of the body help you see, hear, smell, taste, and touch? Draw lines to show your answers.

I see with my

I hear with my

I smell with my

I taste with my

I touch with my

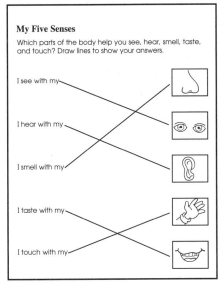

163

## My Eyes

Draw a picture of your eyes.

Pictures will vary.

Color the things you like to see. Answers will vary.

164

## My Ears

Draw a picture of your ears.

Pictures will vary.

Color the things you like to hear. Answers will vary.

165

## My Mouth

Draw a picture of your mouth and teeth.

Pictures will vary.

Color the things you like to eat. Answers will vary.

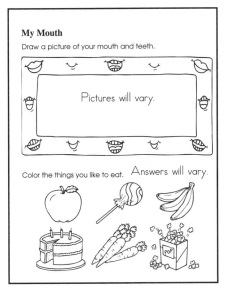

166

## My Hands

Draw a picture of your hands.

Pictures will vary.

Color the things you like to touch. Answers will vary.

167

## I Brush My Teeth

Circle the things that you use to brush your teeth.

Draw a picture of yourself brushing your teeth.

Pictures will vary.

Brush your teeth,
Clean and floss,
Show those cavities
Who s the boss!

168

## I Am Growing

_____ Answers will vary.

I weigh _____ pounds.

I am _____ inches tall.

Color the things that help you grow.

169

## I Eat Healthful Snacks

Circle six healthful snacks.

170

**Let's Eat Dinner!**

Read each sentence. Draw a line to the matching picture.

I will eat spaghetti.

I will eat green beans.

I will eat bread.

I will eat a cupcake.

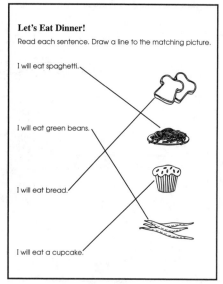

173

**My Favorite Food**

Finish the sentence. Draw a picture to match.

My favorite dinner meal

is    Answers will vary.

My favorite drink is

Here is what I like to eat for dinner.

174

**Plant at Work**

Cut out the pictures. Match and paste them in order.

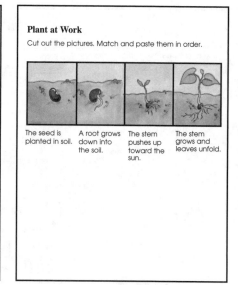

The seed is planted in soil.

A root grows down into the soil.

The stem pushes up toward the sun.

The stem grows and leaves unfold.

175

**Plant Fun**

Find the word in each row. Color the boxes to show the word.

seed

root

stem

dirt

sun

water

leaf

| s | e | e | d | x |
|---|---|---|---|---|
| b | r | o | o | t |
| s | t | e | m | p |
| d | i | r | t | l |
| a | s | u | n | k |
| w | a | t | e | r |
| t | l | e | a | f |

177

**Parts of a Plant**

Trace the words and the lines. Color the plant.

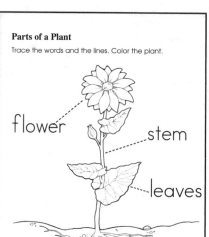

flower

stem

leaves

roots

178

**Eating Plants**

Trace the words.

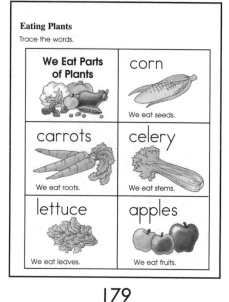

We Eat Parts of Plants

corn
We eat seeds.

carrots
We eat roots.

celery
We eat stems.

lettuce
We eat leaves.

apples
We eat fruits.

179

**At the Market**

Look at the picture. Find **3** foods. Write their names.

oranges

toys

mom

cereal

baby

apples

cart

1. oranges

2. apples

3. cereal

180

**Plants We Eat**

Circle the words. The words go → and ↓,

| k | p | u | m | p | k | i | n | l |
|---|---|---|---|---|---|---|---|---|
| c | i | f | n | u | c | l | a | e |
| e | l | f | s | c | a | r | r | o | t |
| l | y | b | r | g | d | q | d | t |
| e | m | p | c | o | r | n | w | u |
| r | o | v | z | m | v | j | h | c |
| y | e | b | e | a | n | s | r | e |

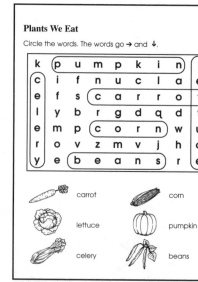

carrot

corn

lettuce

pumpkin

celery

beans

181

*Essential Skills and Practice Grade K*

**Plant Groups**

Cross out the plant in each box that does not belong.
Color the other plants.

182

**Trees Give Many Gifts**

Circle the pictures that show ways people use trees and
things that come from trees.

183

**A Special Garden**

Draw a picture of yourself standing in a garden.

Pictures will vary.

Describe what you see standing in the garden.

I see _Answers will vary._
I hear _____
I smell _____
I feel _____

184

**Garden Days**

Circle and write the best title for each picture.

A Long Nap
No More Weeds
Smell the Flowers

No More Weeds

A Sweet Lunch
A Big Bird
Trees Are Green

A Sweet Lunch

185

**Out of Place**

Circle 1 thing in each box that does not belong.
Answer the question at the bottom.

Everything circled is a kind of what? _food_

186

**In the Forest**

Look at the picture. Find 3 living things.
Write their names.

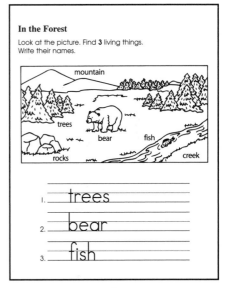

1. trees
2. bear
3. fish

187

**At the Farm**

Look at the picture. Find 3 living things.
Write their names.

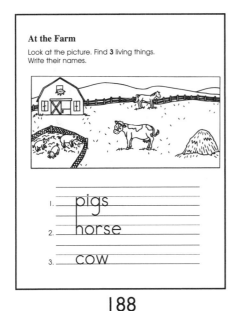

1. pigs
2. horse
3. cow

188

**Pets We Like**

Color the pictures. Say the words. Check off the pets
you have or would like to have.

☐ turtle        Answers        ☐ bird
               will vary.
☐ snake                        ☐ dog
☐ cat                          ☐ rabbit

189

*Essential Skills and Practice Grade K*

**How Animals Move**

Tell how each animal moves. Trace the words.

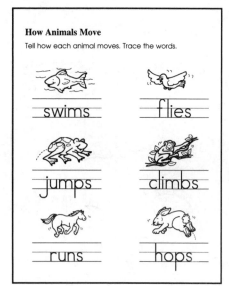

swims          flies

jumps          climbs

runs          hops

190

**Flying High**

Color the things that fly.

191

**I Want My Mommy!**

Trace the line from each baby to its mother.

192

**Little Lost Lamb**

Help the lamb find its mother.

193

**Mrs. Cow's Friends**

Trace the names of Mrs. Cow's barnyard friends. Color.

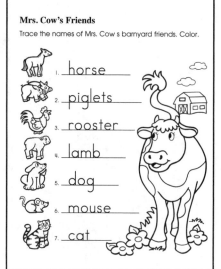

1. horse
2. piglets
3. rooster
4. lamb
5. dog
6. mouse
7. cat

194

**Search and Find**

Find the objects in the woods. Color them.

deer    eggs    squirrel    fish    frog    snake

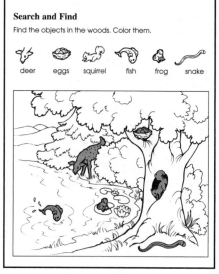

195

**A Beaver Family**

Help the beavers get out of their house.

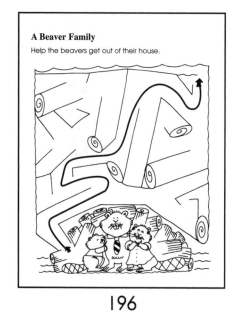

196

**The Zoo**

Finish each sentence with the name of an animal.

bear          monkey          snake          zebra

I see a    bear

I see a    monkey

I see a    snake

I see a    zebra

197

### Hear Me Roar!

Connect the dots from 1 to 10. Color.

198

### Where Are the Tigers?

Help the boy find his way to the tigers.

199

### Train Safari

Help the train take the right path through the forest. Watch out for elephants!

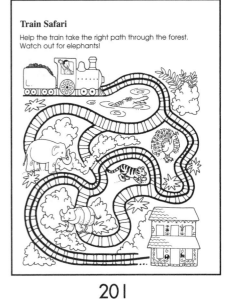

201

### Rain Forest Animals

Look at the picture. Read the words. Write the words on the lines.

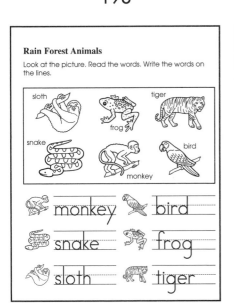

202

### What's Wrong?

In each picture, cross out the part that cannot really happen. Color the pictures.

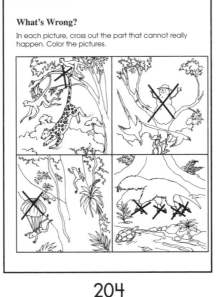

204

### Ocean Animals

Write each animal's name in the correct place.

206

### Fishy Friends

Help the striped fish swim through the coral and find its friend.

207

### Beautiful Birds

Circle the words. The words go → and ↓.

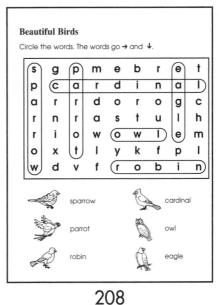

208

*Essential Skills and Practice Grade K*

### A Bunch of Butterflies
Color the butterfly that is different.

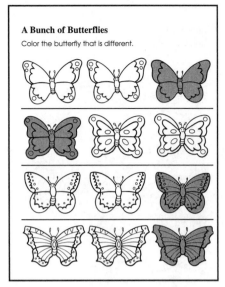

**210**

### Go Buggy!
Unscramble each word. Use the Word Bank for help. Write the words in the puzzle.

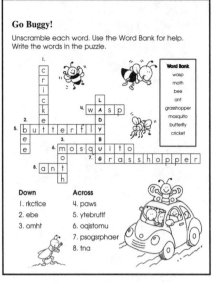

**Word Bank**
wasp
moth
bee
ant
grasshopper
mosquito
butterfly
cricket

**Down**
1. rkctice
2. ebe
3. omht

**Across**
4. paws
5. ytebrutlf
6. oqistomu
7. psogsrphaer
8. tna

**211**

### Bug Walk
Show the bug how to cross the leaf.

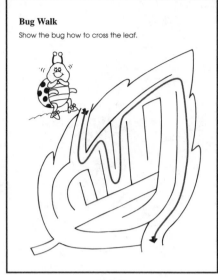

**212**

### A Bunch of Beetles
Find the **3** beetles that match. Color them.

**213**

### Where Is My Home?
Trace each path. Color the pictures.

**214**

### Animal Sightings
Cut out each animal card below on the dotted lines. Glue each card under the picture of where you find the animal.

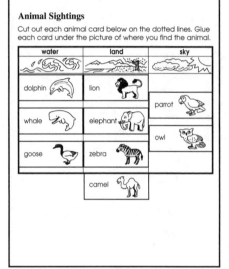

| water | land | sky |
|---|---|---|
| dolphin | lion | parrot |
| whale | elephant | owl |
| goose | zebra | |
| | camel | |

**215**

### A Long Time Ago
Color the scene. Then trace the letters below.

Dinosaurs lived a
long time ago.

**217**

### Maiasaura Maze
Some dinosaurs made nests on the ground. They laid eggs in the nests. Baby dinosaurs hatched from the eggs.

Can you help Mother Maiasaura get back to her nest? Draw a line to show her path. Watch out! T-Rex wants to eat her.

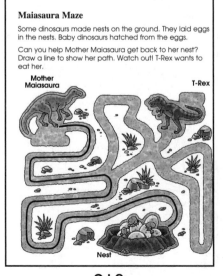

**218**

## Long Gone

Connect the dots from 1 to 25. Color.

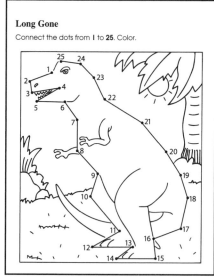

**219**

## Plant-Eater or Meat-Eater?

Some dinosaurs ate meat. Some dinosaurs ate plants. Look at the pictures. Circle yes or no to answer the questions.

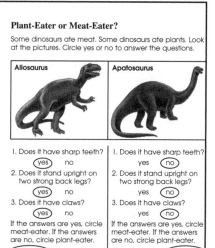

| Allosaurus | Apatosaurus |
|---|---|

1. Does it have sharp teeth?
   (yes)   no

1. Does it have sharp teeth?
   yes   (no)

2. Does it stand upright on two strong back legs?
   (yes)   no

2. Does it stand upright on two strong back legs?
   yes   (no)

3. Does it have claws?
   (yes)   no

3. Does it have claws?
   yes   (no)

If the answers are yes, circle meat-eater. If the answers are no, circle plant-eater.

(meat-eater)   plant-eater

If the answers are yes, circle meat-eater. If the answers are no, circle plant-eater.

meat-eater   (plant-eater)

**220**

## Seasons

Color the pictures. Trace and say the season words.

winter   spring
summer   fall

**221**

## Spring, Summer, Fall, Winter

Number the events in order. Write a number in each box. Then color the pictures.

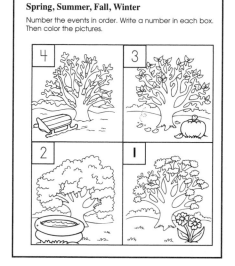

**222**

## Fall Scramble

Unscramble the fall word on each leaf. Color the leaf the correct color.

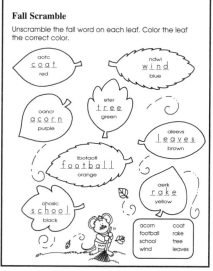

aotc
c o a t
red

ndwi
w i n d
blue

eter
t r e e
green

oancr
a c o r n
purple

aleevs
l e a v e s
brown

lbotaofl
f o o t b a l l
orange

aerk
r a k e
yellow

ohoslc
s c h o o l
black

| acorn | coat |
| football | rake |
| school | tree |
| wind | leaves |

**223**

## Winter Word Search

Circle each winter word from the word box in the puzzle. Check off each word as you find it. Words go across and down.

□ flakes   □ blizzard   □ sled   □ cold
□ skate    □ snow       □ snowman □ freeze
□ January  □ ice        □ mittens □ ski

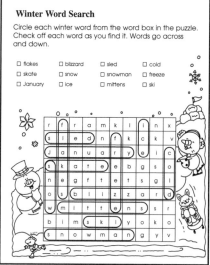

**224**

## How Is the Weather?

Trace and color.

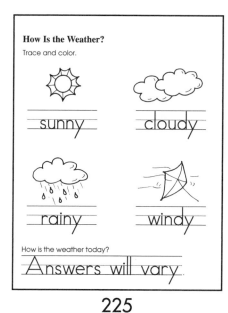

sunny   cloudy
rainy   windy

How is the weather today?

Answers will vary

**225**

## Weather Words

Circle the words. The words go → and ↓.

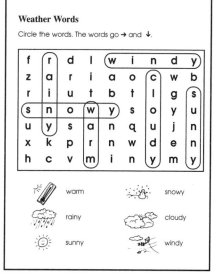

warm     snowy
rainy    cloudy
sunny    windy

**226**

**Cold or Warm?**

Look at the clothes each child is wearing.
Circle **cold** if the child is dressed for cold weather.
Circle **warm** if the child is dressed for warm weather.

227

**How Does It Feel Outside?**

Write a word for each picture.

| hot | warm | cold |

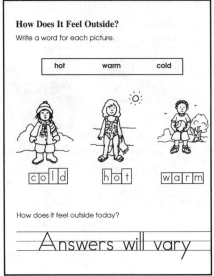

c o l d     h o t     w a r m

How does it feel outside today?

Answers will vary

228

**Rain or Shine**

Look at each weather forecast on the left and draw a line to show what the girl should wear.

229

**Off to Space!**

Connect the dots from 1 to **25**. Color to finish the picture.

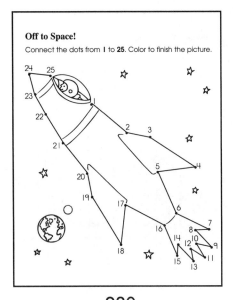

230

**Far Out!**

Circle the words. The words go → and ↓.

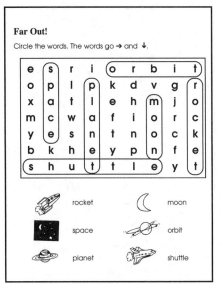

rocket
moon
space
orbit
planet
shuttle

231

**My Name**

Write your name.

First name

Answers will vary

Middle name

Last name

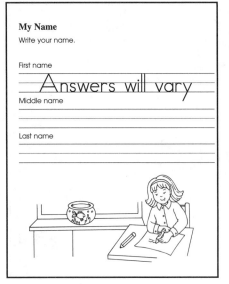

232

**Baby Days**

Draw a picture of yourself when you were a baby.

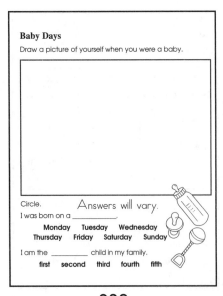

Circle.     Answers will vary.
I was born on a _____.
**Monday   Tuesday   Wednesday
Thursday   Friday   Saturday   Sunday**

I am the _____ child in my family.
**first   second   third   fourth   fifth**

233

**Happy Birthday**

Draw candles to show how old you are.

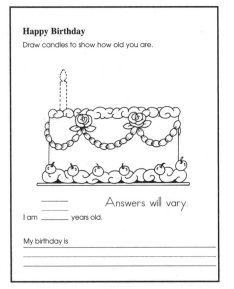

_____     Answers will vary.
I am _____ years old.

My birthday is
_____

234

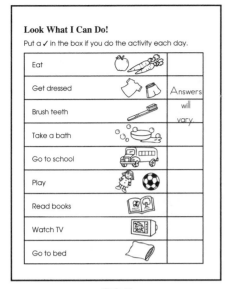

**Look What I Can Do!**

Put a ✓ in the box if you do the activity each day.

| | | |
|---|---|---|
| Eat | | |
| Get dressed | | Answers will vary |
| Brush teeth | | |
| Take a bath | | |
| Go to school | | |
| Play | | |
| Read books | | |
| Watch TV | | |
| Go to bed | | |

235

**Getting Bigger Each Day**

Color the things that you can do now. Circle the things that you want to learn to do. Continue on the next page.

Answers will vary.

236

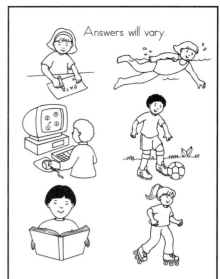

Answers will vary.

237

**My Favorite Toy**

Draw a picture of your favorite toy.

Answers will vary.

Color other toys you like.

239

**My Family Laughs!**

Draw a picture showing something that makes your family laugh.

Pictures will vary.

Color the things that make you laugh.

Answers will vary.

240

**I Can Get Mad**

Color the pictures that make you feel mad.

241

**I Get Scared** Answers will vary.

Color the pictures of things that scare you.

242

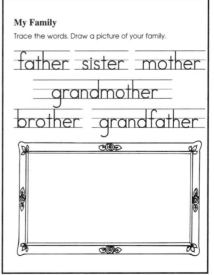

**My Family**

Trace the words. Draw a picture of your family.

father sister mother
grandmother
brother grandfather

243

*Essential Skills and Practice Grade K*

**We Do Things Together**

Look at each picture. If your family likes to do what is shown, color the picture.

Answers will vary.

244

Answers will vary.

245

**My Jobs**          Answers will vary.

Color the pictures of the jobs you do.

246

**When I Am Older**     Answers will vary.

Color the pictures of the jobs that you would like to do someday.

247

**I Play Inside**

Color the things you could play with inside.
Draw an X on the things you could not play with inside.

248

**Indoor and Outdoor Fun**

Color the things you use inside yellow. Color the things you use outside blue.

outside     inside     outside

outside     inside     outside

outside     inside     inside

249

**My Friends**

Draw a picture of two of your friends.

My friends names are _____ Answers will vary

and _____

We like to _____

250

**Friends Are Polite**

Look at each picture.
Write the polite sentences next to the matching pictures.

Say this if you ask for something.

Please.

Say this if your friend gives you something.

Thank you!

Say this if you hurt your friend s feelings.

I m sorry.

251

**Friends Have Fun**

Draw a line to the picture that completes the sentence.

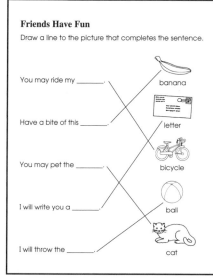

You may ride my _____.

Have a bite of this _____.

You may pet the _____.

I will write you a _____.

I will throw the _____.

banana

letter

bicycle

ball

cat

252

**Chef Charlie**

Chef Charlie tossed the pizza crust. Where did it go?

253

**When I Grow Up**

Color the pictures that show what you might be when you grow up.

Answers will vary.

254

When I grow up, I want to be a

Answers will vary

255

**Learning the Past**

Help the museum guide find the dinosaur display.

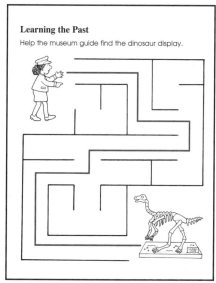

256

**To the Rescue**

Connect the dots from **A** to **Z**. Color.

257

**Places**

Draw lines to show where each item belongs.
Say the names of the places.

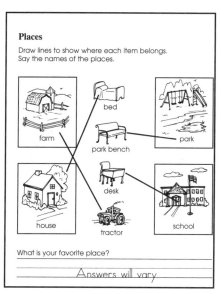

farm

bed

park

park bench

house

desk

tractor

school

What is your favorite place?

Answers will vary

258

**A Busy Day**

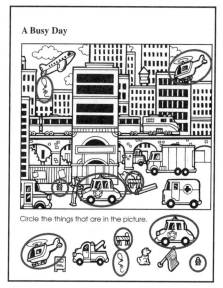

Circle the things that are in the picture.

259

*Essential Skills and Practice Grade K*

**Off to School**

Connect the dots from **A** to **Z**.

260

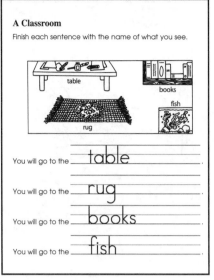

**A Classroom**

Finish each sentence with the name of what you see.

table

books

fish

rug

You will go to the **table** .

You will go to the **rug** .

You will go to the **books** .

You will go to the **fish** .

261

**School Time**

Color the pictures. Check off the boxes of the things you do at school.

☐ sing

Answers will vary.

☐ draw

☐ count

☐ paint

☐ read

☐ write

262

**Playground Fun**

Trace the words.

swing

climb

slide

kick

What do you like to do at the playground?

Answers will vary.

263

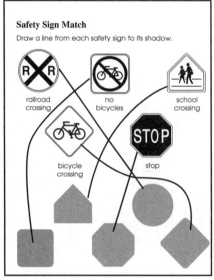

**Safety Sign Match**

Draw a line from each safety sign to its shadow.

railroad crossing

no bicycles

school crossing

bicycle crossing

stop

264

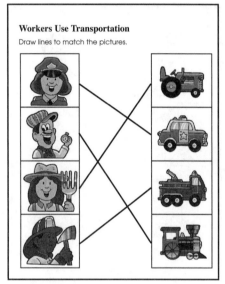

**Workers Use Transportation**

Draw lines to match the pictures.

265

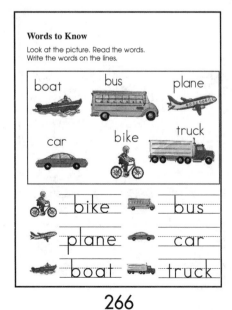

**Words to Know**

Look at the picture. Read the words. Write the words on the lines.

boat

bus

plane

car

bike

truck

bike

bus

plane

car

boat

truck

266

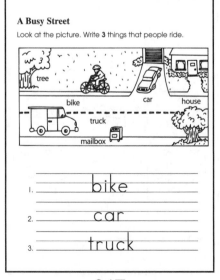

**A Busy Street**

Look at the picture. Write **3** things that people ride.

tree

bike

car

house

truck

mailbox

1. bike

2. car

3. truck

267

*Essential Skills and Practice Grade K*

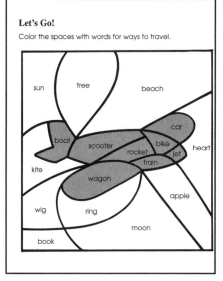

**Let's Go!**
Color the spaces with words for ways to travel.

sun | tree | beach
boat | scooter | car
kite | rocket | bike | jet | heart
train
wagon
wig | ring | apple
book | moon

268

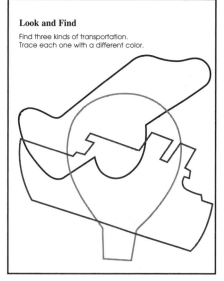

**Look and Find**
Find three kinds of transportation.
Trace each one with a different color.

269

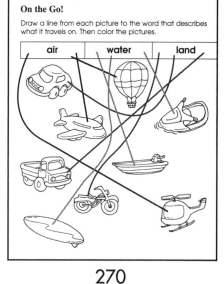

**On the Go!**
Draw a line from each picture to the word that describes what it travels on. Then color the pictures.

air | water | land

270

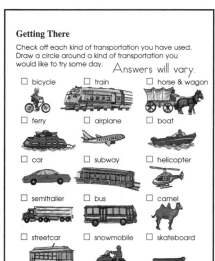

**Getting There**
Check off each kind of transportation you have used.
Draw a circle around a kind of transportation you would like to try some day. Answers will vary.

☐ bicycle   ☐ train   ☐ horse & wagon
☐ ferry   ☐ airplane   ☐ boat
☐ car   ☐ subway   ☐ helicopter
☐ semitrailer   ☐ bus   ☐ camel
☐ streetcar   ☐ snowmobile   ☐ skateboard

271

**Going on a Trip**
Where would you like to go on a trip? Draw it.
Trace and finish the sentence.

I will go to
Answers will vary.

272

Answers will vary.
Color the things that you will take on your trip.

273

**Away We Go**
Circle and write the best title for each picture.

The Big Plane
Trains Are Fun
(Going to Camp)

Going to Camp

A Snowy Day
(On Our Boat)
At the Zoo

On Our Boat

274

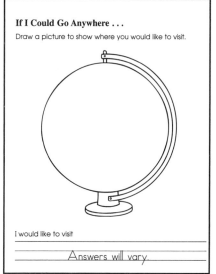

**If I Could Go Anywhere . . .**
Draw a picture to show where you would like to visit.

I would like to visit
Answers will vary.

275

*Essential Skills and Practice Grade K*

## Halloween Puzzle

Read each clue. Write the correct word in the puzzle space

**Down**
1. You wear me.
3. I taste good on apples.
4. I spin my own home.

**Across**
1. I am made of apples.
2. What you say on Halloween
   is _____-or-treat
5. I grow on a tree.
6. You get me on Halloween.

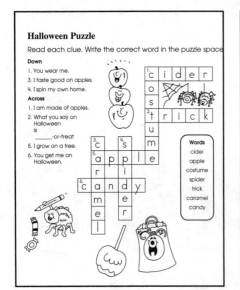

**Words**
cider
apple
costume
spider
trick
caramel
candy

276

## Search for Spring Holiday Words

Circle each spring word in the word search.
Check off each word on the list as you find it in the puzzle.
Words go across and down.

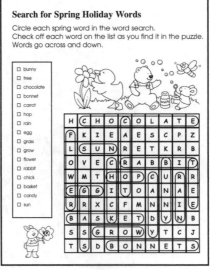

- bunny
- tree
- chocolate
- bonnet
- carrot
- hop
- rain
- egg
- grass
- grow
- flower
- rabbit
- chick
- basket
- candy
- sun

279

## Don't Litter

Color the picture of the seashore. Then put a big **X** on all the trash that should go in the trash can. There are five pieces of trash.

282

## City or Village Life

Color the pictures that show city life **blue**. Color the pictures that show village life **orange**. Color the pictures that can be village or city life **red**.

| | |
|---|---|
| red | blue |
| blue | red |
| orange | red |
| orange | blue |
| orange | blue |

283

## Mountain Maze

One of Maria s chores is collecting reeds for weaving baskets. Help Maria find her way through the mountain trails to get to the river bank where the reeds grow.

284